John Henry Parker

The Archaeology of Rome

Vol. 1 Part 2

John Henry Parker

The Archaeology of Rome
Vol. 1 Part 2

ISBN/EAN: 9783337377922

Printed in Europe, USA, Canada, Australia, Japan

Cover: Foto ©ninafisch / pixelio.de

More available books at **www.hansebooks.com**

THE
ARCHÆOLOGY OF ROME.

BY

JOHN HENRY PARKER, C.B.

HON. M.A. OXON., F.S.A. LOND. ;

KEEPER OF THE ASHMOLEAN MUSEUM OF HISTORY AND ARCHÆOLOGY, OXFORD,

VICE-PRESIDENT OF THE OXFORD ARCHITECTURAL AND HISTORICAL SOCIETY,

AND OF THE BRITISH ARCHÆOLOGICAL SOCIETY OF ROME ;

HONORARY MEMBER OF VARIOUS ARCHÆOLOGICAL SOCIETIES,

ENGLISH AND FOREIGN.

VOL. I. PART II.

ILLUSTRATIONS TO

I. THE PRIMITIVE FORTIFICATIONS.
II. THE WALLS AND GATES OF ROME.
III. THE HISTORICAL CONSTRUCTION OF WALLS.

OXFORD:
JAMES PARKER AND CO.

LONDON:
JOHN MURRAY, ALBEMARLE-STREET.
1874.

CONTENTS.

PRIMITIVE FORTIFICATIONS.

PLATES

Description of the Plans and Diagrams . . . . I.—IV.

Description of the Views . . . . . . I.—IV.

Appendix—Description of the Photo-Engravings of the Hills of Rome: the Palatine, the Viminal, the Cœlian, the Aventine . I.—XXII.

WALLS AND GATES OF ROME.

Description of the Diagrams . . . . . I.—VIII.

Description of the Photo-Engravings . . . . I.—XI.

CONSTRUCTION OF WALLS.

Description of the Plates . . . . . . I.—XVIII.

Appendix—Mamertine Prison, &c. . . . XIX.—XXII.

Capitolium, &c.—Details of Construction . . . I.—IV.

Description of the Diagrams of the Capitolium, containing the Ærarium, Tabularium, Senaculum, and Municipium . . I.—VIII.

DESCRIPTION OF THE PLANS AND DIAGRAMS

OF THE

PRIMITIVE FORTIFICATIONS.

PRIMITIVE FORTIFICATIONS—PLANS AND DIAGRAMS.

PLATE I.

GENERAL PLAN OF ROME, with the Walls of the Kings, of Aurelian, and of the Popes.

In this small Plan the hills are tinted grey, and the valleys left white, with the streams of water flowing through them, green; the Walls of the Kings are tinted red; that of Aurelian, with the towers, is solid black; that of the Leonine City and the Hadrianum, a thick black line; and that of the Popes in black outline.

This plan, with the section above, was taken originally from what was considered as the best geological plan of Rome. But it does not profess to be a geological plan in its present form, it is only intended to give a general idea of the nature of the ground on which the City of Rome stands, in the valley of the Tiber. The Seven Hills have probably all been originally promontories, from the high table-land on each side. The three COLLES, the Quirinal, Viminal, and Esquiline, clearly are so, and the Janiculum and Vatican on the western side.

PLATE 1.

GENERAL PLAN OF ROME,
WITH THE WALLS OF THE KINGS, AURELIAN, AND THE POPES.

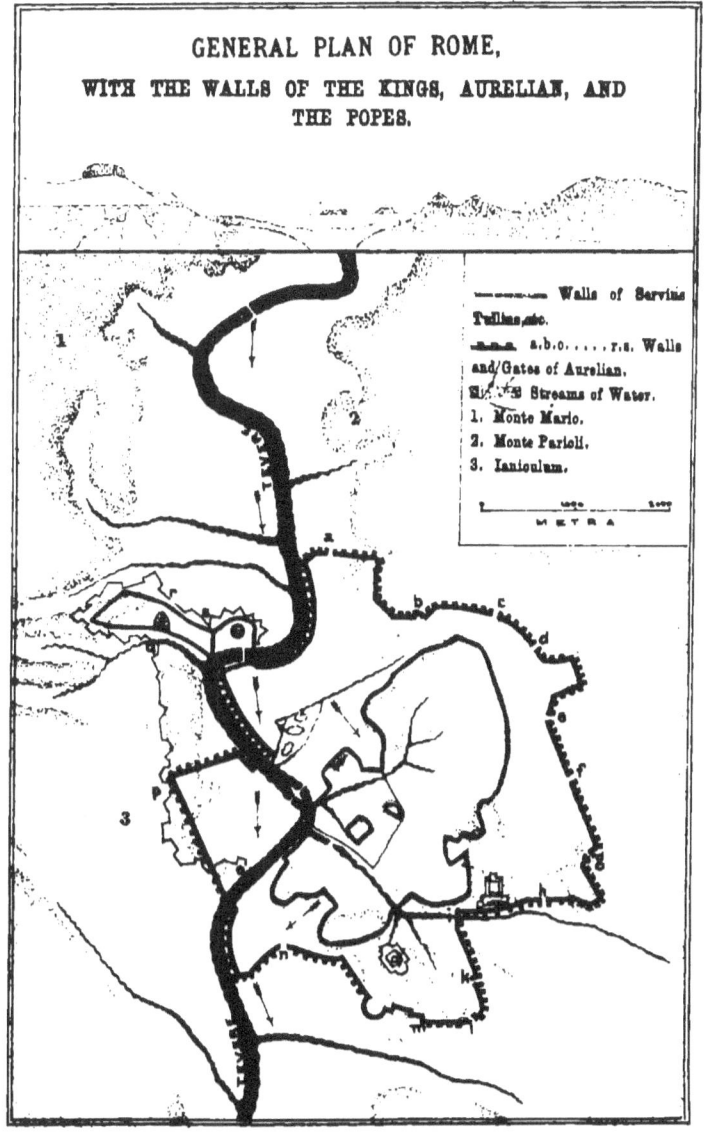

PRIMITIVE FORTIFICATIONS—PLANS AND DIAGRAMS.

PLATE II.

ROMA PRIMITIVA. The object of this Plate is to give a more clear idea of the original *City of Rome*, both of the first and second period. The first City consisted of the Palatine Hill only, of which the northern part was more strongly fortified than the rest. This strongest part, or citadel, was an oblong space on the side next the Hill of Saturn, of which the Sabines were then in possession, and were for a time at war with the Romans. This space, called *Roma Quadrata*, was the *arx*, citadel, or keep of the Palatine City. It may have been called *Quadrata* either from its oblong form, or because it was surrounded by walls built of large oblong blocks of tufa, of the construction called by Vitruvius *Opus quadratum*. It had a triple line of defence round it at different levels, as was usual for the *arx*. Remains of the wall against the upper cliff are now visible on three sides. This wall is distinguished on the plan by a solid red line where it is now visible, and by a dotted red line where it has been destroyed, but must have gone. On the south, the west, and the north, parts of the wall remain against the cliff; on the south side is the great foss across the middle of the hill, called by some a natural valley, or *intermontium;* it was probably partly natural, but certainly only in part, with the cliffs supported by walls on both sides of the great foss. The Porta Mugionis is near the east end of this foss, the approach to it protected by the cliffs on both sides spreading out in a gorge as usual. *The second City* consisted of the two hills, the Palatine and the Hill of Saturn inclosed in one wall, which is also marked by a red line, solid where it remains, and in dots only where it must have passed. It must have included the Velia at the east end, to protect the approach to the principal gate, and have gone to the Tiber on the south-west in order to keep open that highway for provisions. The tufa wall of the second period against the bank of the Tiber, called the *Pulchrum Littus*, must have formed part of this line of defence, and the small river Almo may also have formed a wet ditch for a certain distance. The other streams and marshes in the valleys added greatly to the strength of the Palatine fortress, before they were collected in the great drain, called *Cloaca Maxima*.

PLATE II.

ROMA PRIMITIVA.
WALL OF PALATINE AND CAPITOL COMBINED IN ONE CITY.

PAVED ROADS ━━━━━ WATER ━━━━

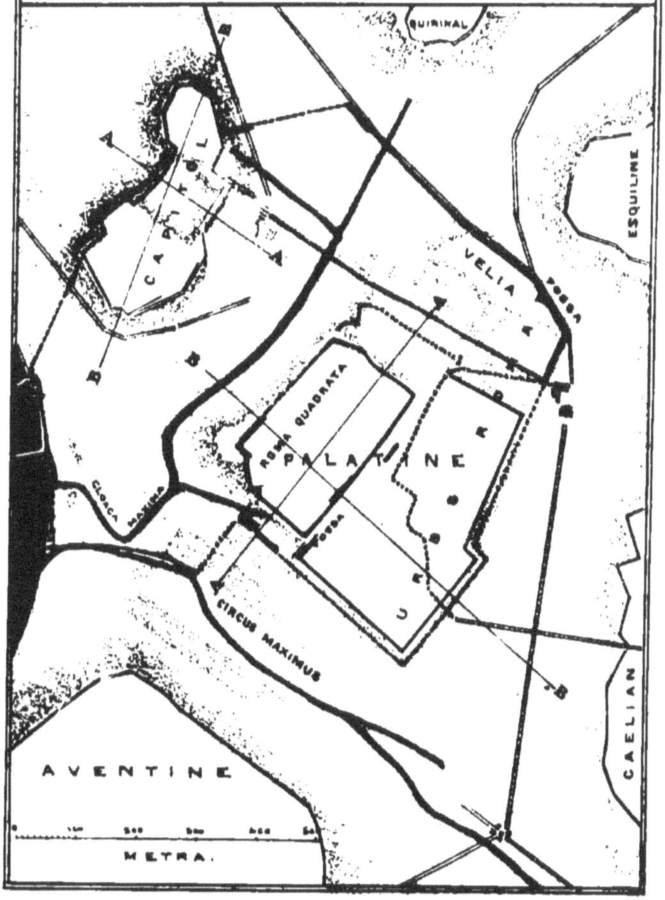

PRIMITIVE FORTIFICATIONS—PLANS AND DIAGRAMS.

PLATE III.

DIAGRAM OF THE PALATINE HILL, WITH A SMALL PORTION
OF THE CAPITOLINE.

THIS Plate contains a section of a portion of the Capitoline Hill, with a plan of the Via di Marforio, a narrow street at the foot of it, on the eastern side, with some excavations made there in the spring of 1872, shewing the junction of the *agger* and wall of the second City with the rock of the Capitol. This is on a line with the south end of the Forum of Trajan, and goes across to the great wall at the foot of the Quirinal. Immediately outside of, and to the north of the *agger*, was part of the great foss in which the Forum of Trajan was partly made, and which extended to this point, as is shewn by remains of it in the cellars of the houses. About a hundred feet north of the *agger* is the tomb of Bibulus, which originally stood on the side of the foss or trench on the outer bank or *vallum*, this was usually a burial-place in the Etruscan cities.

The lower part of the plate gives longitudinal and transverse sections of the Palatine Hill, in which the vertical scale is made double that of the horizontal one, to make it more clear in a small space. The red walls against the cliffs at different levels shew the positions of the remains of these early walls. The valley (or *intermontium*) across the middle of the hill is also indicated.

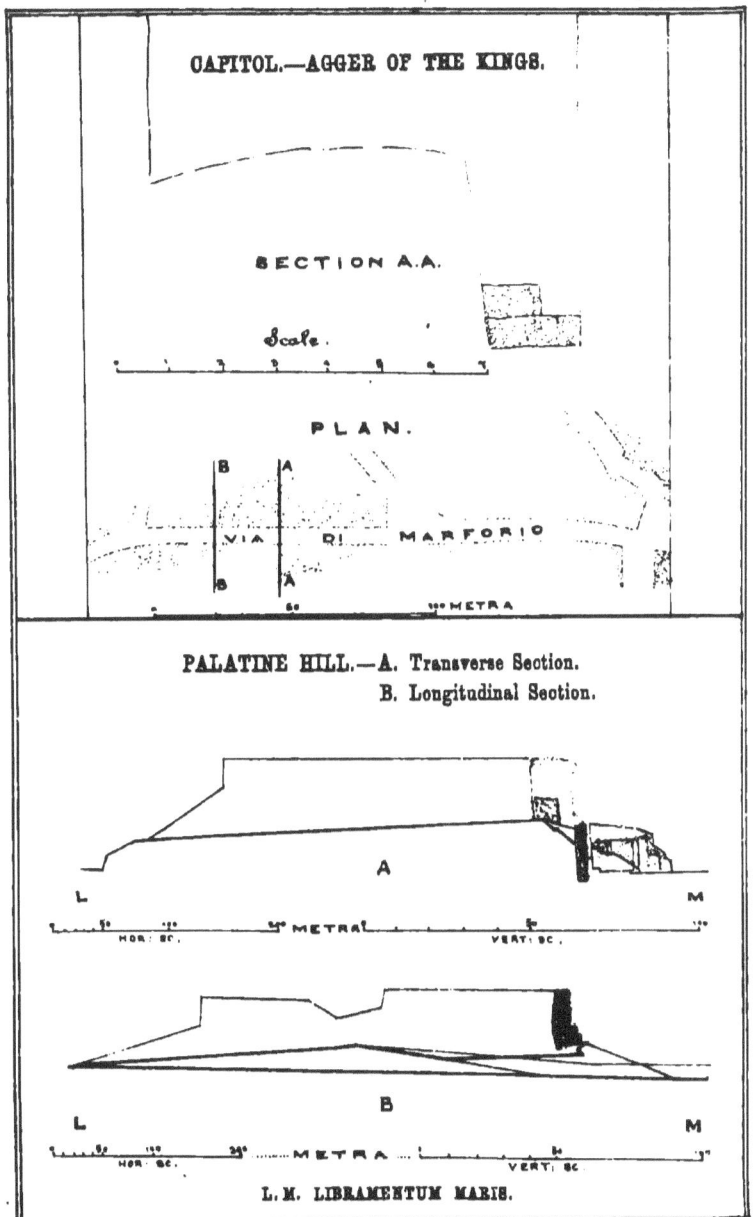

PRIMITIVE FORTIFICATIONS—PLANS AND DIAGRAMS.

PLATE IV.

SECTIONS, LONGITUDINAL AND TRANSVERSE, OF THE CAPITOLINE HILL, OR HILL OF SATURN, A and B. This is intended only to give a general idea of the form of the Capitoline Hill, or Rock, with the zigzag road up to the summit on the northern side, which was restored in 1872, and in doing so part of the scarped cliff of the original fortress was brought to light.

SECTION C, of the VELIA, with portions of the Palatine and Esquiline, shewing that the Velia was originally a promontory from the Esquiline Hill, cut off by a great foss at some very early period. This great foss is seen to the right in the section, it is now the Via del Colosseo. Persons standing on the steps of a small church near the north end of this great foss, and looking south towards the Colosseum, can see the trees growing on the level of the ground twenty feet above the present level of the road, made in the foss: the earth is supported by a wall against the cliff on each side. The other foss seen towards the left of the section is the *clivus*, or inclined road from the Colosseum to the Arch of Titus, which stands upon the Summa Via Sacra. The red vertical lines indicate the site of Walls of the Kings, or of scarped cliffs, with or without a wall to support them. The buildings indicated on this section are the Arch of Titus, and the church of S. Francesca Romana; the Lavacrum of Heliogabalus, excavated in 1872, is also indicated under the cliff of the Palatine, near the Arch of Titus.

PLATE IV.

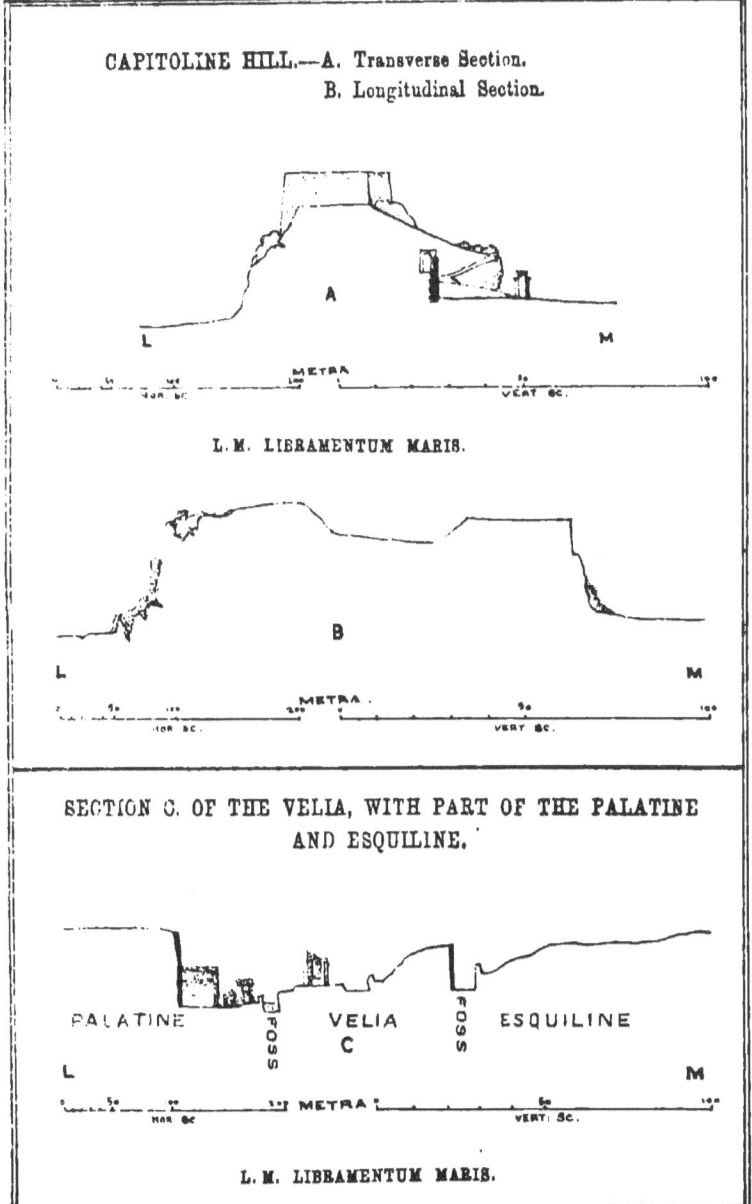

DESCRIPTION OF THE VIEWS

OF THE

PRIMITIVE FORTIFICATIONS.

PRIMITIVE FORTIFICATIONS—VIEWS.

PLATE I.

GENERAL View of the north-west corner of the Palatine Hill, shewing the most perfect part of the Wall of Romulus, or of Roma Quadrata, with buildings of the time of the Republic and of the Empire built upon it and against it, and supported in places by modern brickwork.

Beyond this wall of *Opus quadratum* is seen a lofty wall of Concrete, with deep grooves in it, both vertical and horizontal, in which a timber framework has been left to rot, and these grooves have remained. This is said to be the earliest concrete wall in Rome, built at a time when the builders had no faith in the strength of lime-mortar, and therefore depended on their wooden framework for the support of the cliff.

PRIMITIVE FORTIFICATIONS. PALATINE. N. W.

PRIMITIVE FORTIFICATIONS—VIEWS.

PLATE II.

THE Wall of Roma Quadrata in detail, shewing the width of the joints and the rude construction. The wide vertical joints are the characteristic feature of the walls of the first period in Rome, of the time of the early Kings. They occur on the Palatine Hill only, [in the walls of Roma Quadrata]: there are remains of them on three sides of an oblong space at the north end of this hill, in the part nearest to the hill of Saturn, which was occupied by the Sabines at the time that these walls were built.

A photograph of the wall of the Etruscan cities of Fiesole or of Volterra, taken on the same scale as this, would be almost identical with it.

PRIMITIVE FORTIFICATIONS, PALATINE. N.-W. DETAILS

PRIMITIVE FORTIFICATIONS—VIEWS.

PLATE III.

REMAINS of a Tower, the two sides of which are seen with a concrete wall of the time of the Republic between them, shewing that it was left unfinished, the part built being used as a foundation for another building. This tower is immediately opposite to the hill of Saturn at the nearest point, and just within reach of stones thrown by catapults from that hill. This was proved by some experiments tried by M. Viollet-le-Duc for Napoleon III. at Pierrefonds. He had a catapult made to try how far it would throw a paving-stone, and he found that it would just throw one far enough to have knocked down a Roman in his hut at this point. This tower is one of a series along this end of the hill, begun and left unfinished, and subsequently used as foundations for later buildings.

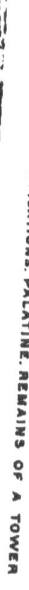

PRIMITIVE FORTIFICATIONS. PALATINE. REMAINS OF A TOWER

3

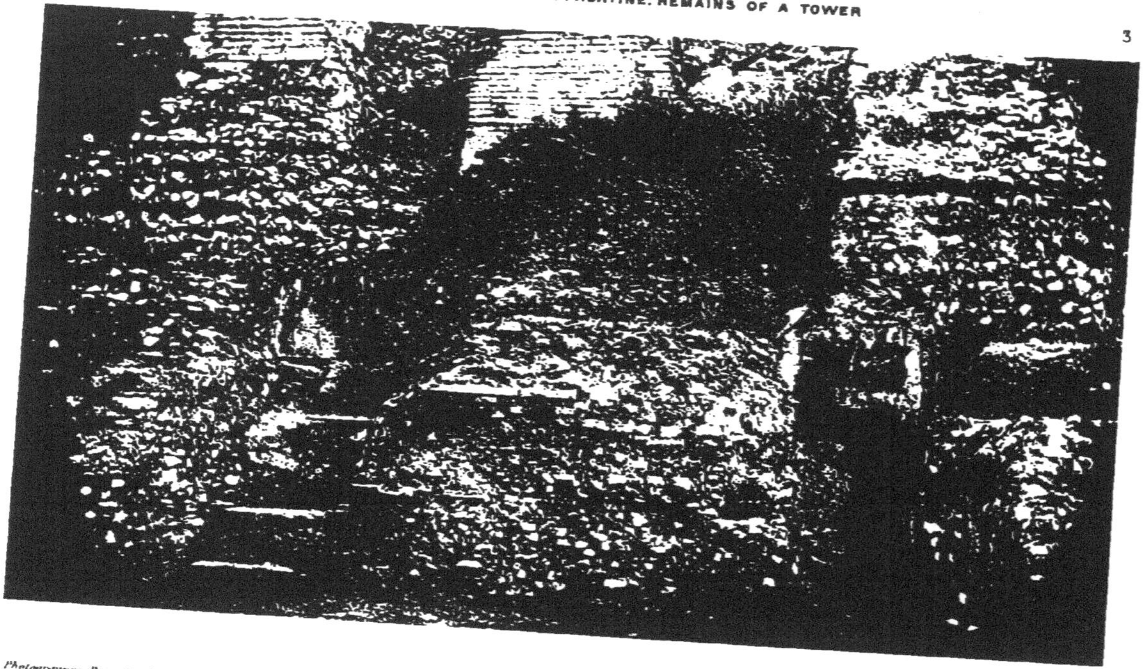

Photogravure Dujardin, Paris

PRIMITIVE FORTIFICATIONS—VIEWS.

PLATE IV.

CŒLIAN HILL. South-west corner, shewing the scarped cliff of the original keep, when that hill was a separate fortified village; and the wall of the Claudium built up against it. Against the wall there are also remains of an *Exedra*, or place for seats for some public exhibition, probably, from the situation, the Ludus Magnus. The wall built up against the cliff is of the time of the early Empire, and it is hollow, having a space of about two feet wide in it, in order to keep the seats dry, and prevent the moisture from the earth behind passing through the wall. Sometimes these hollow spaces are wider, and are used for a passage. The Claudium is a square space at the north-east corner of the Cœlian Hill, with vertical cliffs on three sides of it, and the sloping road called the Clivus Scaurus on the south. The Arch of Dolabella is near the south-west corner of it, on the road leading into it from the east. On the other side a porticus or arcade of the time of Claudius remains against the cliff. This has probably been a double arcade, one over the other, although we have only part of the lower one now remaining; the whole square space above would probably be inclosed by an arcade, in the centre of which was the Temple of Claudius.

Round a temple of importance there was frequently an area or space enclosed by a wall, against which was a porticus or arcade, and the porticus was frequently a double arcade one over the other. In this instance the lower arcade was built against the cliff to support it, the upper one would face towards the temple, and afforded a shady retreat in hot weather. The marks of the arches of the lower arcade against the cliff are here distinctly visible.

PRIMITIVE FORTIFICATIONS, COELIAN: S.W. OF CLAUDIUM

APPENDIX TO THE CHAPTER ON THE PRIMITIVE
FORTIFICATIONS.

DESCRIPTION OF THE PHOTO-ENGRAVINGS

OF THE

HILLS OF ROME.

THE PALATINE.

HILLS OF ROME.

THE PALATINE.

PLATE I.

TEMPLE OF JUPITER FERETRIUS, and Podium, or basement of the same; the construction of the walls of this temple are identical with that of the outer walls, of the large squared stones of *Opus quadratum*, with the wide vertical joints, which are found nowhere else in Rome but at this north end of the Palatine Hill. The temple of Jupiter Feretrius is recorded by Livy to have been built in the year iv. of Rome, to commemorate the first conquest of the Romans, that of Antemnæ, and we might therefore expect to find, as we do, the construction the same as that of the walls, as is shewn in these engravings. Roman topographers have been misled by the name of *Capitolium*. Livy states that this temple was built *in Capitolio* (Livii Hist., i. 10), but in the year four of Rome the Romans had not possession of the Hill of Saturn, which was occupied by the Sabines, and the great public building called *Capitolium* was not then built. The capitol or keep of the Romans *at that time* was Roma Quadrata, on the north end of the Palatine Hill. Vitruvius says that the house of Romulus was in the Capitol, yet other authors distinctly describe it as on the Palatine Hill. His words may be thus translated:—"The house of Romulus *in the capitol*, by its thatched roof, clearly manifests the simple manners and habits of the ancients." (Vitruvius, " Ancient Architecture," bk. ii. ch. 1.)

PALATINE HILL

TEMPLE OF JUPITER FERETRIUS

PODIUM OF TEMPLE

HILLS OF ROME.

THE PALATINE.

PLATE II.

TEMPLE OF JUPITER FERETRIUS, another part, and the STEPS OF CACUS leading up to it from the site of the Circus Maximus, and from the Pulchrum Littus on the banks of the Tiber. The construction of these steps is exactly the same as that of the walls.

The gigantic steps of Cacus are among the earliest legends of Roman history, and the notices we have of their site agree exactly with those lately excavated. They are expressly said to have led to the Tiber. These also lead down to the platform on which the house of Romulus is recorded to have stood, and it appears natural that this communication would be made from his house to the first temple that he built. A communication from the citadel to the Tiber was also very important, as that river was the high road for the supply of provisions for the garrison. The construction, being exactly the same as that of the earliest wall, is a strong confirmation of what was otherwise probable, and when the existing remains agree in this manner with the traditions of the people and with probability, they amount almost to history. The words of Solinus are very explicit, and exactly fit this locality :—" Roma Quadrata . . . begins in the area of Apollo, and terminates at the brow of the steps of Cacus, where stood the hut of Faustulus, where Romulus dwelt, who laid the foundation of these walls [a]." These steps are on the brow of the hill near which also this temple stands, and they lead down from the temple to the platform on which the house of Romulus stood, according to Vitruvius [b], Diodorus [c], Plutarch [d], and others, (now just behind the church of S. Anastasia,) which is just over the Lupercal.

In the lower view, which shews the *Podium*, or basement of the temple, an arcade is also seen in the background; this belongs to one of the palaces of the Cæsars, and is supposed to have been used for stables; it is work of the first century, but not of the time of Caligula, to which it is commonly attributed.

[a] Solinus, c. i. v. 18.
[b] Vitruvius, lib. li. c. 1.
[c] Diodorus, lib. iv. c. 21.
[d] Plutarch, Romulus, c. 20.

PALATINE HILL

STEPS OF CACUS

HILLS OF ROME.

The Palatine.

Plate III.
House of Hortensius and Augustus.

The situation of this house so exactly agrees with the description of Suetonius and Dion Cassius, that there can be no hesitation in considering it as identified, more especially as the construction of the walls also agrees perfectly with that period. They are all faced with *Opus reticulatum*, or net-work, and that kind of net-work which was in use at that time, in which the diamond-shaped blocks were larger, and the mortar between them thicker, than it was at a later period; the walls are of the time of Sylla. The house is divided into two parts, the original house of Hortensius consisting of small chambers, exactly like houses of the same period at Pompeii; and in this part there is no ornament. The other part, consisting of chambers of more than double the size, and each of the height of two storeys of the original house; and in these state apartments, evidently added on to the original house, there are fine mosaic pavements and fresco paintings of the time of Augustus. These details are clearly shewn in the two plates. A plan and section of the house is given among the diagrams on Plates V. and VI.

MINE HILL

PALATINE HILL

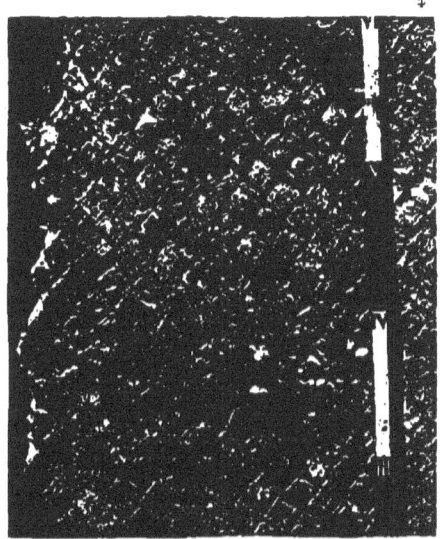

HOUSE OF HORTENSIUS

HOUSE OF HORTENSIUS AND AUGUSTUS

HILLS OF ROME.

The Palatine.

Plate V.*
Plan of the House of Hortensius and Augustus.

The small chambers at the top of the plan are those of the house of Hortensius, that of an ordinary citizen, as at Pompeii of the same period. The large chambers below on the plan are state apartments of Augustus, erected by order of the Senate, in which are fine mosaic pavement and fresco paintings, but the house of Hortensius was quite plain. The steps leading down into the Atrium, or central open court, of the state apartments, for the use of the public, are seen on the left-hand corner of the plan; they lead from a long corridor, which passes from the eastern side of the hill, and communicates with other corridors or passages running north and south. The subterranean passages on the Palatine are very numerous, some of them were for the private use of the emperors, from their palaces to the state apartments in the middle of the hill. The small narrow private steps for the use of Augustus descending from the private house (originally the house of Hortensius), are seen on the right of the plan, and in the centre of the Cavædium, or covered court of the house; other steps are seen which now lead to nothing, but led originally to an upper storey, which was of wood; only a narrow passage divides the original "house of an ordinary citizen" from the shops which are between it and the street, shewn by the pavement. The upper storey, of wood, probably extended over the passage and the shops, which have no steps, and therefore had no room over them, nor cellars under them. The underground storey of the house of Hortensius has only been partially excavated, so that we cannot tell whether the cellars extended under the shops or not. Another narrow passage, seen at the top of the plan, leads from the house to the middle of the hill, and to other reservoirs of water all underground. The floor of the cellar of the underground storey is level with that of the state apartments added, which were of the height of two original storeys. The great oval water-reservoir was added afterwards, it is miscalled a *piscina*, Frontinus would have called it a *castellum aquæ*. It was supplied with water by the Anio Novus of Nero, no other aqueduct would reach to that high level.

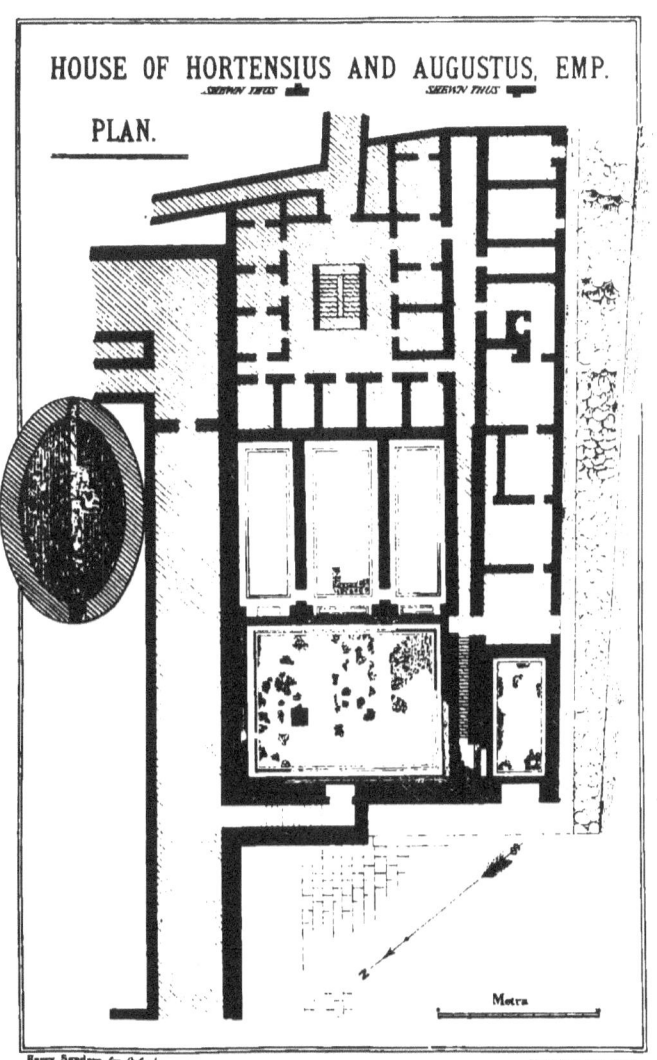

HILLS OF ROME.

THE PALATINE.

PLATE VI.*

SECTIONS OF THE HOUSE OF HORTENSIUS (A) AND AUGUSTUS (B). In the original house of Hortensius (A), which was the house of an ordinary citizen of that period (as we are told by Suetonius), the rooms were all small, as in similar houses of the same period at Pompeii, and the rubble walls are faced with the reticulated work in use at that time. This is separated from the additions made to the house by order of the Senate (as we are told by Dion Cassius) by a wall of the same construction, in which there is neither door nor window.

The additions (B) made to the house in which Augustus persisted in residing (and where we are told that he slept for forty years), were intended for state apartments for the use of the Emperor, and contained rich mosaic pavements and the finest wall-paintings of the period. Although they are of very moderate dimensions compared with the state apartments of Domitian, half a century afterwards, in the middle of the Palatine, this is only in accordance with what we are told of the modest pretensions of Augustus, and his desire to live the life of a private gentleman.

HOUSE OF HORTENSIUS (A) AND AUGUSTUS, EMP. (B). SECTIONS.

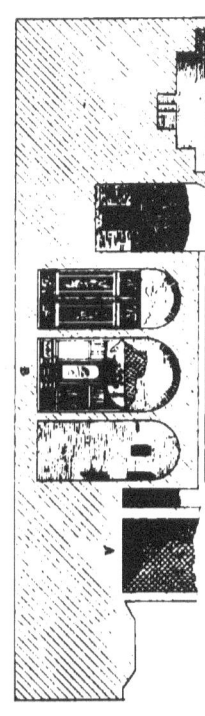

SECTIO C.D. DOMUS HORTENSII (A) ET AUGUSTI (B).

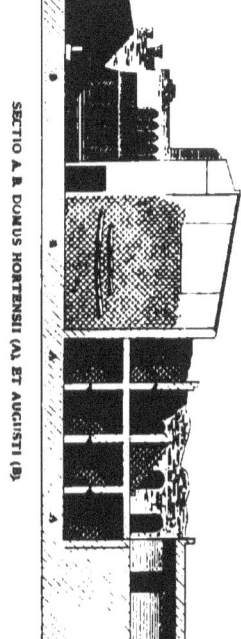

SECTIO A.B. DOMUS HORTENSII (A) ET AUGUSTI (B).

HILLS OF ROME.

THE PALATINE.

PLATE V.

THE LUPERCAL OR WOLF'S CAVE—PLAN AND SECTION.

This shews the natural cave, with the streams of water gushing into it from under the tufa rock of the Palatine Hill, at the north-west corner, with the chambers built up against it by Augustus. The situation of it is near the corner of the Circus Maximus, or in modern times under part of the Via de' Cerchi, at the corner of the Via de' Fienili.

A. is the well, which is the only present approach to it.

B. is the door from one chamber to the other, of brick, of the time of Augustus.

C. is the channel for water, or aqueduct of the Aqua Argentina, which had its source here, and is a beautifully clear stream, running only as far as the Cloaca Maxima, near the Arch of Janus, where it falls into that stream.

The cave is at too low a level to have been accessible to the Romans from the Citadel above, they would have been exposed to the enemy on the opposite hill, and within reach of arrows, or of stones thrown from a catapult. For this reason a reservoir for rain-water was made above, at the north-west corner of the wall of Roma Quadrata, shewn in the next plan.

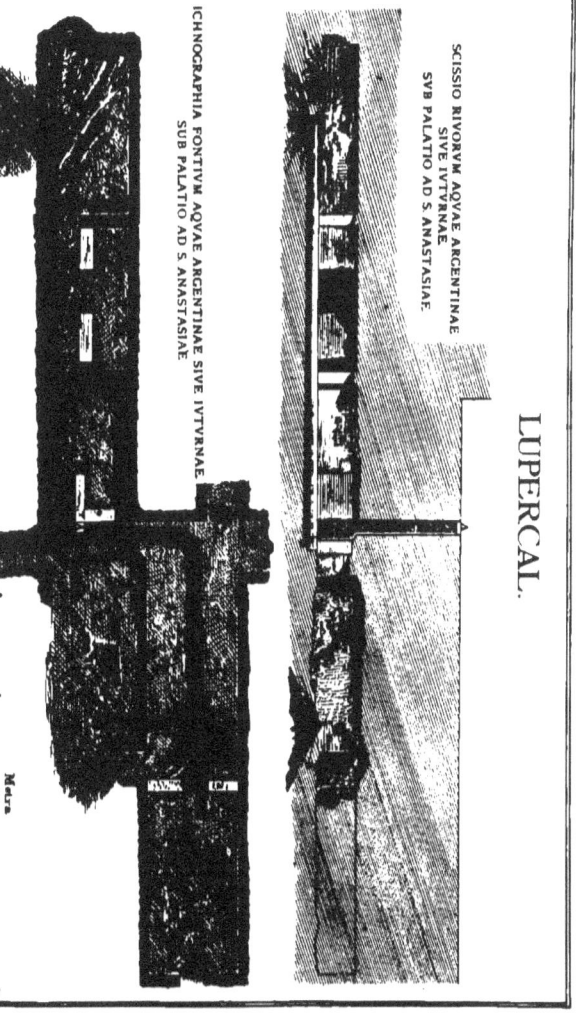

HILLS OF ROME.

The Palatine.

Plate VI.

1. Section of a Reservoir for rain-water, of the time of Romulus, at the north-west corner of the Palatine, and of the Citadel, or *Roma Quadrata*, behind the most perfect part of the wall of that period that remains. There are three channels to bring water to this cave-reservoir from different parts of the hill, and through the rock which forms a vault over it are three wells of a peculiar form, a sort of hollow cone shewn in the drawing.

2. The lower portion is a similar reservoir for rain-water at Alba Longa, under the corner of the *arx* or Citadel there, now occupied by the small monastery called Palazzuola. This also has a well of the same form, and these are the only two examples of wells of that form that are known in this part of Italy.

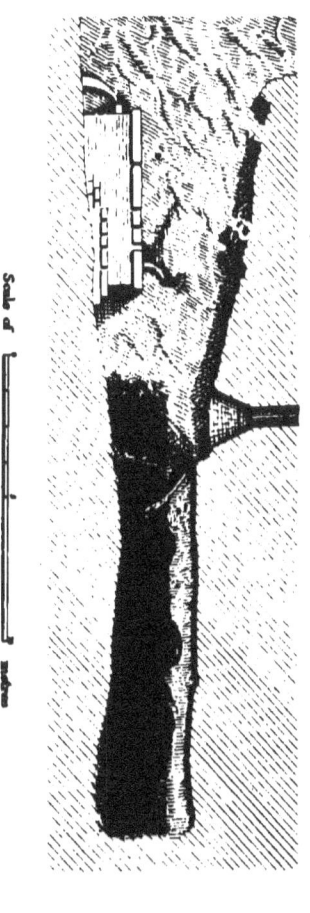

RESERVOIR OF WATER AT THE NORTH-WEST CORNER OF THE PALATINE (ROMULUS).

RESERVOIR OF WATER AT PALAZZUOLO (ALBA LONGA?).

HILLS OF ROME.

THE PALATINE.

PLATE VII.

HOUSE OF AUGUSTUS AND TIBERIUS.

Domus Augustana et Tiberiana (Curiosum Urbis et Notitia, Reg. X.) These two houses, or palaces, are mentioned together in the Regionary Catalogue, because they stood together. The back of the house of Tiberius almost joins on to the western side of the house of Hortensius and Augustus. The front of it was on the cliff towards the Circus Maximus, that is, on the Germalus, and near to the Velabrum. This front fell down in a landslip in the last century, (probably caused by the ground having been undermined by ignorant people living in the lower road); the backs of the chambers built against the cliff remain, and the construction of the walls is identical with that of the interior of the northern wall of the Prætorian Camp, built by Tiberius; in all which particulars it agrees exactly with the history we have of it. Tiberius being the adopted son of Augustus, this was a natural arrangement. Tacitus mentions (in Hist. i. 27) that Otho passed by the palace of Tiberius to the Velabrum, and this was the obvious way to go from the temple of Apollo above. There were steps through the palace of Tiberius from the level of the summit of the hill to that of the platform, behind the seats in the gallery of the Circus Maximus, and on this platform was the road from the southern end of the Palatine to the Velabrum. The palace, called by modern topographers that of Tiberius, is on the northern angle just above the Forum Romanum, and joining on to that of Caligula. But the latter was on the lower level, and close to the Forum, and had the temple of Castor and Pollux as a vestibule to it. The upper palace is of the time of Trajan and Hadrian, as shewn by the construction of the walls.

CONSTRUCTION — OPUS RETICULATUM — NET-WORK.

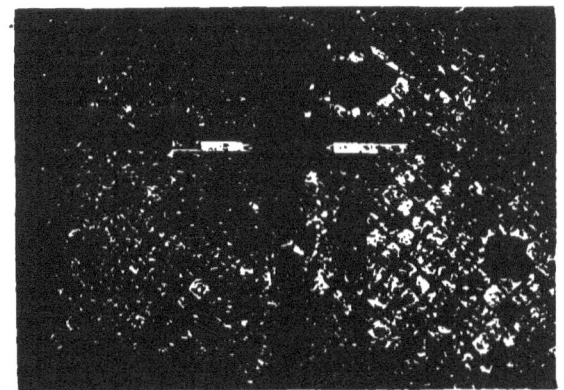

HOUSE OF HORTENSIUS. B.C. 50.

PALACE OF TIBERIUS. A.D. 20.

HILLS OF ROME.

THE PALATINE.

PLATE VIII.

PALACE OF CALIGULA, A.D. 40. The construction of this is not quite so good as that of Nero, but there is very little difference, it is extremely good. This palace is at the foot of the hill, at the corner near the Forum Romanum, and joined on to the temple of Castor and Pollux, which served for a vestibule to it (Suetonius in Caligula, c. 22); (the placing it on the top of the hill is therefore a mistake). His celebrated bridge went from this palace at the west end of it, across the west side of the Forum Romanum to the temple of Jupiter Capitolinus, on the top of the Tarpeian rock on the opposite hill; two of the piers of the bridge remain joining on to the palace, at the west end, and almost forming part of it.

PALACE OF TRAJAN, A.D. 100, and HADRIAN, A.D. 120, on the Palatine Hill. These are in fact part of one great public building on the top of the hill at the north-east corner, much above and nearly over that of Caligula, and miscalled by his name. The work that was carrying on in the time of Trajan was somewhat altered in the time of Hadrian, as the ideas of the Senate were enlarged. The square brick pier, shewn on the left-hand side of the view is of the time of Hadrian, built up against the wall of Trajan, and was made to carry a lofty vault over the paved road or street called the Via Triumphalis. This vault seems to have been an after thought, the piers to carry it are not bonded into the wall of Trajan, but carried up from the ground. It often happened at all periods that the vaults were additions, there has first been a wooden roof only, and then a vault introduced.

CONSTRUCTION — OPUS LATERITIUM — BRICK-WORK.
18

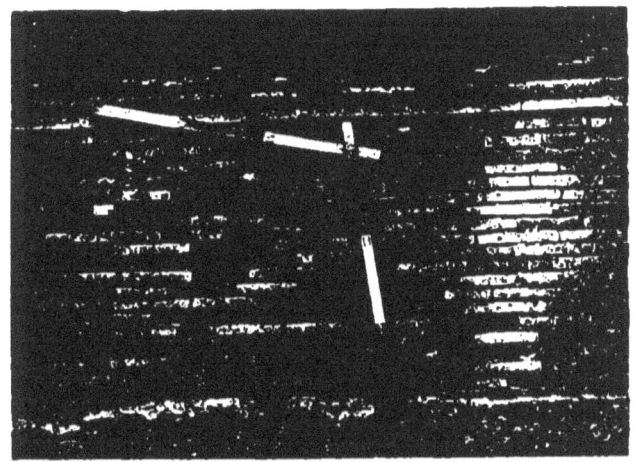

PALACE OF CALIGULA A.D. 40.

PALACE OF TRAJAN AND HADRIAN, OVER THE VIA TRIUMPHALIS? A.D. 100-120.

Photogravure Dujardin, Paris

HILLS OF ROME.

THE PALATINE.

PLATE IX.

PALACES OF THE CÆSARS. — THE REMAINS OF THE PALACE OF DOMITIAN. These are built upon the site of the great foss on the south side of Roma Quadrata. Transverse walls were built across the foss at short intervals, and vaults across from one wall to the other, in order to raise a level platform at the original level of the ground, so that the whole of these great public palaces might be on one level, with subterranean passages and chambers under them. These transverse walls are from fifteen to twenty feet high, and are cut through other buildings previously erected in the foss, without scruple. One of these (now subterranean) chambers is called a bath-chamber of Julia, because it has a fine painted vault of the time of Augustus; this is on the low level of the bottom of the foss, and not here visible. The construction of the walls is of the time of Domitian, whose brick-stamps have also been found in them. This was part of the grand design of the Senate mentioned by Dion Cassius, as being formed in the time of Augustus, for covering the whole of the Palatine Hill with a series of public palaces, and as time went on, and the Roman empire extended, the ideas of the Senate became more and more magnificent. All these palaces of the Cæsars are in fact public buildings, erected at the cost of the State, and an inscription has been found upon them to that effect. The great Basilica was the central point. It was the State Hall for grand occasions, where the Emperor sat in state to distribute honour to the officers on their return from a successful campaign. What are seen in these two views are chiefly the remains of the great Basilica of the Cæsars, called the BASILICA JOVIS, the height of which is shewn by one angle of it, which appears in each of the views on different sides, and fragments of the short columns, of which there were two tiers. The remains are slight but interesting, and the views shew exactly the present state of this part of the Palatine Hill, after the recent excavations of the Emperor Napoleon III., and of the Italian Government who purchased the ground of him, and continued the excavations under the same superintendence, of Signor Rosa.

HILLS OF ROME.

THE PALATINE.

PLATE X.

REMAINS OF THE PALACE OF DOMITIAN. These two views are in the same great basilica, called the BASILICA JOVIS, the principal state-hall of the Palatine, the place for all the grandest ceremonies of the Roman Emperors, and at the same time, like the English House of Lords, the highest court of justice. The ground-plan is not altered, and can be clearly seen, with the apse at the east end, and remains of the seat of the Emperor on the wall, and the perforated marble screen across the chord of the apse: at the north-east corner, that portion of the wall which forms the angle still stands at its original height, and the remains of the two rows of columns which divide the hall into a nave or aisles, shew that they were only half the height of the building, and that there were galleries there, as mentioned in Vitruvius. The fragments that remain are slight, but interesting, and extremely picturesque. In the Church of S. Agnes, which is a good copy of the Basilica type, and which was built in the fourth century, the galleries remain, and are still in use.

PALACES OF THE CAESARS ON THE PALATINE

REMAINS OF THE PALACE OF DOMITIAN

HILLS OF ROME.

THE VIMINAL.

PLATE XI.

REMAINS OF TOWERS OF THE ARX AGAINST THE CLIFF. These are believed to be vestiges of the early fortifications, when this hill was a separate fortress, before Servius Tullius had enclosed the seven separate fortresses into one city. There are remains of buildings of the time of the Republic built up against them. To the left of the upper view is seen the entrance to the cave, which was considered as a cave of Mithras when it was discovered in the seventeenth century, as is recorded by Flaminius Vacca. It had been buried again and lost sight of, until it was again excavated in 1871, but it does not agree with the character of the caves of Mithras, which is now well known. One of the real caves of Mithras was discovered about the same time by Father Mullooly, nearly under the Church of S. Clement. The present cave is not large enough, and had probably been an early tomb, perhaps afterwards used as a private bath-chamber belonging to the Lavacrum of Agrippina, which closely adjoined to it. It appears that the *arx* or capitol of the Viminal, as a separate fortress, was at this corner.

PRIMITIVE FORTIFICATIONS - VIMINAL

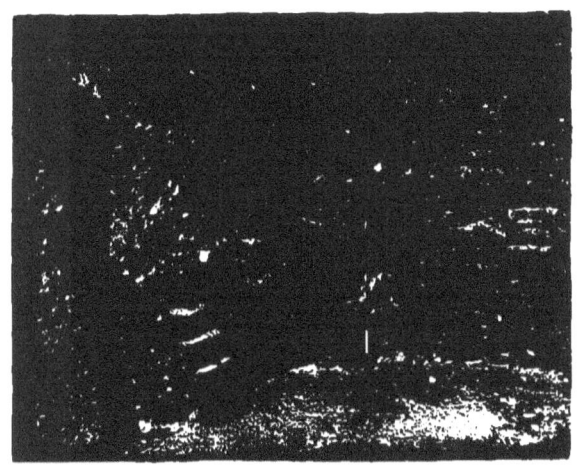

REMAINS OF TOWERS OF THE ARX AGAINST THE CLIFF

HILLS OF ROME.

THE VIMINAL.

PLATE XII.

REMAINS OF THE LAVACRUM OF AGRIPPINA. These are just under the cliff above mentioned, on a lower platform. They were partially excavated by Canina, and inscriptions were then found upon the base of a statue of Bacchus, and on some lead pipes, which identified the building. The excavations were carried further in 1871, and some mosaic pavements and fresco paintings were found. Other pavements had previously been found, but all were soon destroyed by the recklessness of the low inhabitants of the neighbourhood. Another manner in which mosaic pavements of the time of the Early Empire are frequently destroyed in Rome when left open, is by the curiosity of the host of tourists, especially lady tourists, each of whom carries away a few of the tesseræ as mementoes, and as the number of tourists in Rome amounts to many thousands during the season (and it is continually increasing), a piece of tessellated or mosaic pavement is soon destroyed. Exposure to the weather also soon causes weeds to spring up, which displace the tesseræ. The only way to preserve them in their original place is to keep them covered with a thin layer of earth, which can easily be removed when necessary. At one end a wall of brick of the time of Hadrian was found built up against the lavacrum; this is shewn in the upper view, with the arches of construction in the wall.

VIMINAL HILL

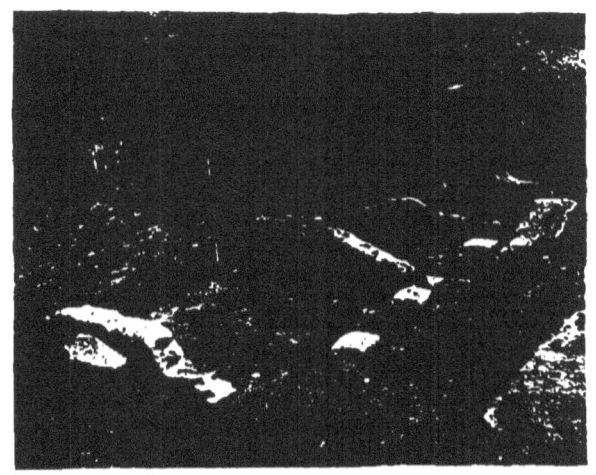

REMAINS OF THE LAVACRUM OF AGRIPPINA

Photogravure Dujardin

HILLS OF ROME.

THE CŒLIAN.

PLATE XIII.

CŒLIAN.—THE ARX.—THE CLAUDIUM, EAST SIDE, WITH WALL OF THE LUDUS MAGNUS, at the south-east corner near the Colosseum. This *arx* has scarped cliffs on three sides and part of the fourth, where it is cut off from the rest of the hill by the deep cutting called the Clivus Scauri, which is the entrance from the west and from the Palatine. The portion here represented is on the opposite side, and has a wall of the Ludus Magnus built up against it, as on the other view from the north-east. The Claudium was built above, on the level platform of this ancient fortress. It appears to have consisted of a quadrangle, the sacred enclosure, on a high level, which had a *porticus* or arcade on all sides, of two storeys, the lower one against the cliff, the upper one above it and open to the area, or court within, in the centre of which stood the temple of Claudius, originally intended by him to have been a temple of Peace, but afterwards called by his name, and dedicated to him as a deified Emperor. There were fountains in the quadrangle, and the great aqueduct of Claudius and Nero terminated there. On some maps the whole space is given as a reservoir of water, but this was a mistake. The *specus* or conduit of the aqueduct remains in the northern wall against the cliff, and leads towards the Colosseum.

PRIMITIVE FORTIFICATIONS. CELIAN. THE ARX

THE CLAUDIUM. EAST SIDE. WITH WALL OF LUDUS MAGNUS

HILLS OF ROME.

THE CŒLIAN.

PLATE XIV.

CŒLIAN, NORTH SIDE. -- AN ANCIENT FORTRESS, now the church and monastery of the Santi Quattro Coronati. It is a bold promontory standing out from the north side of the hill, near S. Clement's. The entrance to the monastery and church is on the top of a steep road or *clivus*, by the side of which the ancient fortifications are very evident, originally a scarped cliff only, but with walls built up against it. The fortress originally protected the south end of the short *agger* of Servius Tullius across the valley, which connected the Cœlian fortress with that of the Esquiline; the wall of the *agger* passes under the altar end of S. Clement's church. In the year 1873, when a new quarter of the city was being built, extensive excavations were made in this part, and the wall of Servius Tullius was found continuing on under the apse of the Church of the Santi Quattro, with other remains of early buildings, some of the time of the Early Empire and others earlier. The medieval monastery has evidently been fortified, and must have been a strong fortress from its commanding position, on the verge of a deep gorge, on the other side of which was the Claudium, and in the valley or gorge between them must have been the Ludus Magnus. The name of this hill is now spelt Celian by the modern Italians, who do not use the diphthong.

AN ANTIENT FORTRESS, NOW THE SANTI QUATTRO CORONATI

PRIMITIVE FORTIFICATIONS, CELIAN, NORTH SIDE

HILLS OF ROME.

THE CŒLIAN.

PLATE XV,

CŒLIAN, SOUTH SIDE.—AN ANCIENT FORTRESS, now the Villa Celi-Montana. This fortress originally protected the approach to the Porta Capena, the southern entrance into THE CITY. The fortress stands at an angle of the hill, and has scarped cliffs on three sides of it, with walls built up against them. The Porta Capena stood a little to the north-west of it. On the eastern side it also protected the approach to another gate, at the end of a gorge, an entrance to the Cœlian fortress itself, near which the Navicella now stands. On this site was one of the Cohortes Vigilum, or barracks for the night-guards. Extensive excavations were made in the garden of the villa in the early part of the present century, and an account was published of the objects found, with a plan of the barracks, which were long and narrow (remarkably similar to the Vicars' Close at Wells, in Somersetshire, a curious coincidence). Room was provided for a considerable number of soldiers or others, but this appears to have been done by a number of small dwellings instead of one large barrack, as was more customary. Many of the objects found are preserved in the garden and offices of the villa.

PRIMITIVE FORTIFICATIONS, CELIAN, SOUTH SIDE

AN ANTIENT FORTRESS, NOW THE VILLA CELI-MONTANA

HILLS OF ROME.

THE CŒLIAN.

PLATE XVI.

CŒLIAN—GORGE, FORT AT AN ANGLE, part of the Villa Celi-Montana. This is another part of the same ancient fortress as the last, which is a promontory on the south-west side of the hill, the end of which is towards the Porta Metronia in the south wall, under which the river Almo enters Rome ; on either side of this is a gorge, cutting deep into the hill, one of which is shewn in the view. The upper and narrow end of the gorge nearly meets in the tongue of land which connects this fortress with the other on the northern side, on which the Claudium was built. The Navicella stands on that tongue of land, and close to the site of the gate of the Cœlian fortress, at the end of the southern gorge. The Arch of Dolabella also stands on this tongue of land, and was the gate to the Claudium, at the end of the gorge on the other side of the hill.

PART OF THE GARDEN OF THE VILLA CELI-MONTANA

HILLS OF ROME.

THE AVENTINE.

PLATE XVII.

SCARPED CLIFF, with the Castle of the Savelli built upon the summit. This is on the side next the Tiber; the cliff is partly natural, but has been scarped in places, and walls of the large squared stones of the time of the Kings' built up against it. There is a zigzag path also down the slope from the castle (now the garden of the monks of S. Sabina), leading originally to the Marmorata and the Porta Trigemina, but the lower part of the path has been cut off to make room for modern buildings. It is shewn in one of Piranesi's engravings as over the mouth of the Aqua Appia; which is in a cave under it; the entrance to it is not quite visible in this view, being too far to the right. This cave is also the one called after Picus and Faunus by some antiquaries, and after Cacus by others. It is the only natural cave known under the Aventine. There are wine-cellars and stone-quarries excavated in different parts, but no other natural cave is known. At the back of this is a natural reservoir of water of some extent, supplied by a spring, and this pure water was added to that of the Appia in the front part of this cave. The aqueduct of Trajan also had its mouth nearly over this cave, at a considerably higher level; and there is a vertical terra-cotta water-pipe descending from it into the front part of this lower cave, as in other parts the later aqueducts made use of the Appia, which was the lowest of all, to carry off the surplus water. Some ancient building is visible to the left of the view, which has been built on the slope, and vaulted, and remains of the vaults are seen: this may have been connected with the aqueduct of Trajan.

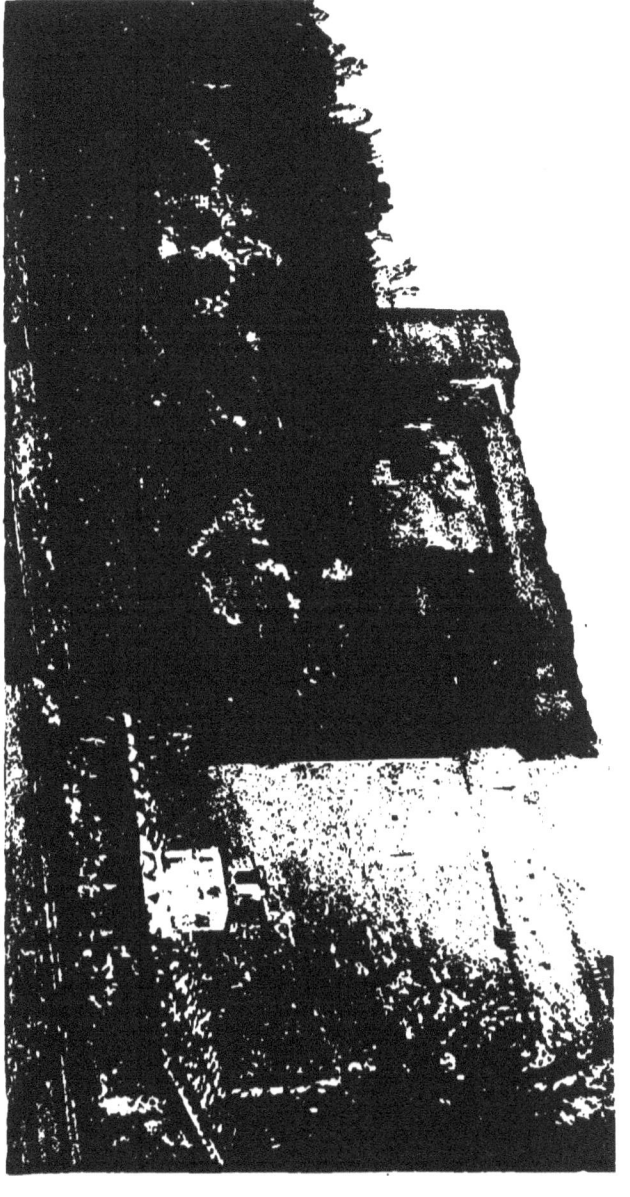

PRIMITIVE FORTIFICATIONS. AVENTINE. SCARPED CLIFF

CASTLE OF THE SAVELLI, BUILT UPON THE CLIFF

HILLS OF ROME.

THE AVENTINE.

PLATE XVIII.

PART OF THE ARX. A scarped cliff under S. Balbina, north side, with Wall of the Kings, &c. The Wall of the Kings is in the centre of the picture, to the right of it are arches of an aqueduct, that of Trajan, which came across the valley from the great reservoir on the Cœlian, over the Arch of Dolabella, and was carried over the Porta Capena before it arrived at this point. A little further on to the right it crosses over the valley between the two parts of the Aventine, and the water was conveyed to that part of the arcade that remains near S. Prisca, and to the Temple of Apollo, now S. Sabina. This interesting portion of the Wall of the Kings, and the *arx* of the Aventine fortress, and of the aqueduct of Trajan, have all been buried, to the depth of ten feet, since this photograph was taken, by the earth thrown here by Signor Rosa, which he had brought from the Palatine in the excavations for the Emperor of the French, thus burying one part of the antiquities of Rome to shew another. If this process had been continued much longer it bid fair to fill up the valley between the two parts of the Aventine, which some think is a great ancient foss only, as there is no natural stream of water through it; but it seems too wide and too deep to be artificial. The part of the hill on which S. Balbina and S. Sabba stand is called the Pseudo-Aventine.

PRIMITIVE FORTIFICATIONS. AVENTINE. PART OF THE ARX.

SCARPED CLIFF UNDER S. BALBINA. NORTH SIDE. WALL OF THE KINGS. ETC.

HILLS OF ROME.

THE AVENTINE.

PLATE XIX.

THE ANCIENT ARX, now the monastery and reformatory of S. Balbina, built upon the old keep of the Aventine fortress, of which the scarped cliffs remain on three sides, mostly concealed by walls built up against them. The present building was at one time the house or castle of the Cardinal, the tower of which is seen in the centre of the picture, over the south side of the castle; the western side is seen to the right of the picture standing upon the Wall of the Kings, which is visible in places on the south-west and north side, and is shewn in other plates. To the left of the picture is a portion of the church of S. Balbina.

The foundations of the tower are of the time of the Kings, a portion of which has been excavated and left open, with a portion of the wall of the ancient fortress going from it towards the other ancient fort under S. Sabba; but these were two distinct fortresses with a long interval between them, as they are at the opposite ends of that part of the hill called the Pseudo-Aventine; the old Via Ardeatina passes between the two, and there was a gate on the hill at this part called the Porta Raudusculana.

PRIMITIVE FORTIFICATIONS, AVENTINE. THE ANTIENT ARX.

MONASTERY OF S. SABINA, BUILT UPON THE OLD KEEP OF THE AVENTINE

HILLS OF ROME.

THE AVENTINE.

PLATE XX.

ANCIENT FORT, with the monastery of S. Sabba built upon it. The high situation of this monastery makes it a very conspicuous object, and the medieval building with the cloister is extremely picturesque. The old fort is seen below the wall, it is built of concrete or rubble-stone in layers, having very much the appearance of having been cast in boxes, like the pier at Dover. It was originally cased with squared stones, some of which were found at the foot of it in the excavations made for the purpose in 1870, and which is seen in one of the photographs. This fort is at the south-west corner of a gorge in the hill, at the narrow end of which is the site of a gate where four roads meet. On the opposite corner, or the south-east angle of this gorge, are considerable remains of another ancient fort, called the Wall of the Latins, shewn in other views. These two forts defended the approach to the gate, when there was no outer wall to this part of the City, and for that reason there was no *pomœrium* to the Aventine until the time of Claudius, who first built an outer wall here.

At the western end of the hill beyond S. Sabba, the city of the Kings and the city of the Empire are identical for a short distance; the wall of the Empire is built up against the lower part of a lofty cliff, which had been scarped, and had formed part of the original fortifications of that hill. From that point to the Tiber the wall of Claudius was built, but it seems to have been a low wall after the old fashion, and was used as foundations for the lofty wall of Aurelian. In the Porta Ostiensis, which is near the cliff, and stands in what was the ancient foss, the two inner gates are of the time of Claudius, the outer one is of Theodoric, who repaired the gateway fortress.

PRIMITIVE FORTIFICATIONS, AVENTINE, ANTIENT FORT

MONASTERY OF S. SABBA, BUILT UPON AN OLD FORT

HILLS OF ROME.

THE AVENTINE.

PLATE XXI.

WALL OF THE LATINS ON THE AVENTINE. A portion with an arch inserted at a later period, but still of an early character; the arch is attributed by the local antiquaries (apparently with reason) to the time of Hannibal, when he rode up to the walls of Rome, and threw his javelin over them in defiance. It is supposed to have served as an embrasure for a catapult. Behind it (as shewn in the upper view) is a mass of concrete, on which a catapult might very well have been fixed. The bed of concrete, with the wall of large blocks of tufa in front of it, is twelve feet thick, and the height of this wall has been measured by dropping down a measuring line, and found to be fifty feet. The wall stands upon a ledge of the tufa rock cut to receive it. In front of it are very remarkable wells, fifty feet deep, on the outer bank of the great foss. These wells appear, on comparing them with similar wells found in Aquitaine, to have been used for the purpose of interment. Cinerary urns, with ashes in them, were found at the bottom of such wells in Aquitaine.

The lower view shews the outside of the arch, and in that part of the wall the insertion is clearly seen. The arches are both of tufa, but not from the same quarry. The wall seems to be made of blocks cut from the rock itself on the spot, the more red kind of tufa comes from a quarry at a short distance only, nearly under the church of S. Prisca.

PRIMITIVE FORTIFICATIONS. AVENTINE

WALL OF THE LATINS ON THE AVENTINE

WALL OF THE LATINS ON THE AVENTINE

HILLS OF ROME.

THE AVENTINE.

PLATE XXII.

PART OF THE THERMÆ OF SURA, the cousin of Trajan, and connected with the Private House of Trajan and his family. The *specus* of an aqueduct, with a triangular head, here seen to the left of the view, passes under the south end of the portion of wall shewn in Plate XXI., and said to be used for a catapult. It is remarkable that the builders of the wall of the Thermæ appear to have been entirely ignorant of the existence of this great Wall of the Kings, which was probably buried in their time, and not visible; for the wall, faced with the reticulated work of the time of Trajan, goes obliquely against the old wall.

The lower view represents this section of the old wall a few yards further on, it is *almost* as early as the wall of Roma Quadrata; as seen in the section it appears to be the same. It has the same wide vertical joints, but on the surface of the wall the joints are closely fitted together. The old wall is part of a fort (now under S. Prisca) to defend the approach to a gate in the time of Servius Tullius, and there is a small fort opposite to it under S. Sabba; only the large blocks which form the facing have been removed for building-materials, excepting underground, where they were found in the excavations made to search for them in 1871. These two forts are at the two angles of a gorge, at the narrow end of which was the gate, and four roads met at that point; or two roads crossed each other, one going from the Porta Ostiensis towards the Palatine, the other along the wall from S. Prisca to S. Sabba. This road is an old *agger*, with the foss on the outside of it.

PART OF THE THERMAE OF SURA

SECTION OF THE WALL OF THE LATINS

WALLS AND GATES OF ROME.

NOTICE ON THE DESCRIPTION OF THE DIAGRAMS.

THESE illustrations will be much more easily understood, and therefore be more useful, by having the description of the plates, with the references to them, placed in such a manner as to face each plate. In order that this may be done without increasing the bulk of the work, it has been thus arranged—
At the back of this leaf is the description of Plate I.
The description of Plate II. is at the back of Plate I.
The description of Plate III. at the back of Plate II., and so on.
In this way the convenience of the reader is consulted in what appears to be the best manner.

The set of thirty-two drawings of the Walls and Gates of Rome, reduced to eight pages, is made by Signor Felice Cicconetti, chiefly from the photographs prepared for this work; but these have been compared upon the spot, and a plan of each portion of the wall or of the gate is added at the foot. As the great Wall of Aurelian is thirteen miles long, it is obvious that the whole extent could not possibly be included, but the parts omitted are those that possess little or no interest, and the distance from one point to another in the intervals is marked by the number of metres (or yards).

This series illustrates the Itinerary of the Pilgrim of the eighth century, known by the name of the "Einsiedlin Itinerary." The pilgrim evidently walked round the walls and jotted down the minute particulars of what he saw and observed as he walked along, and has thus preserved to our day a most exact description of the walls as they then were, which is now extremely curious and interesting. We have followed his steps, and have shewn exactly what now remains of what he then described. It is evident that the foundations are, for the most part, the same, built upon the old earthworks or *mœnia*, and the lower part of the walls remains in many parts. The number of towers between one gate and another can frequently be counted. The upper part of the walls, with the battlements, including the merlons, or upright pieces, and the crenelles, or openings between them, are gone; and the windows, both large and small, have, for the most part, also disappeared; but to this general demolition there are interesting exceptions, there is one tower of Aurelian quite perfect, between the ancient Porta Pinciana and the modern Porta Salaria. The outer wall of the Prætorian Camp is the most perfect part of the walls of Rome now remaining. In this some windows can be seen, both large and small; the framework, made of terra-cotta (see Photograph, No. 12); the battlements also remain perfect in some parts near the north-east corner, with the merlons and crenelles perfect (No. 3001), but built up, as the wall has been raised higher at some early period (No. 3002). The doorway arches frequently have the grooves remaining for the "portcullis gate" to slide up and down; reminding us of the Psalm of David, "Lift up your heads, O ye gates, and the King of Glory shall come in."

I.

1. PORTA FLAMINIA. The present gate is modern, and not exactly on the old site, which was rather more to the left, and eastward, on higher ground (as we are told by Procopius), the line of the road has been carried further out from the cliffs. The tomb of Nero was on the site of the church of S. Maria del Popolo, on the west side of this gate. The building seen to the left of this diagram is the northern part of the great palace of Sylla, to which the celebrated Muro Torto belonged. It was inhabited by Belisarius when he was the general in command of the defence of Rome.

2. The view shews the Muro Torto as seen in profile to the right, where the lower part of the great wall against the cliff of the Pincian Hill was built straight, it now hangs over considerably; the upper part was built upon this after the settlement had taken place, but in a series of niches or semicircular recesses, to throw back the weight of the earth beyond the line of the foundations. To the left of this is the lower part of the western front of the same palace, in which the wall to support the cliff is built in a double series of niches one over the other, apparently because the builders had profited by the experience they had gained on the northern side. All these interesting remains of antiquity are now concealed by a hideous modern wall, the late architect to the municipality of Rome having persuaded them that it was *dangerous*. It had been so considered also in the fifth century, as Procopius mentions.

3. and 4. Shew some of the Towers and Wall of Aurelian, but in this part there is no corridor, as is seen by the plan given under this part, probably on account of the different level of the ground, the wall there being built upon part of the old *mænia*, or earthworks, of the time of the Kings.

WALLS AND GATES OF ROME.

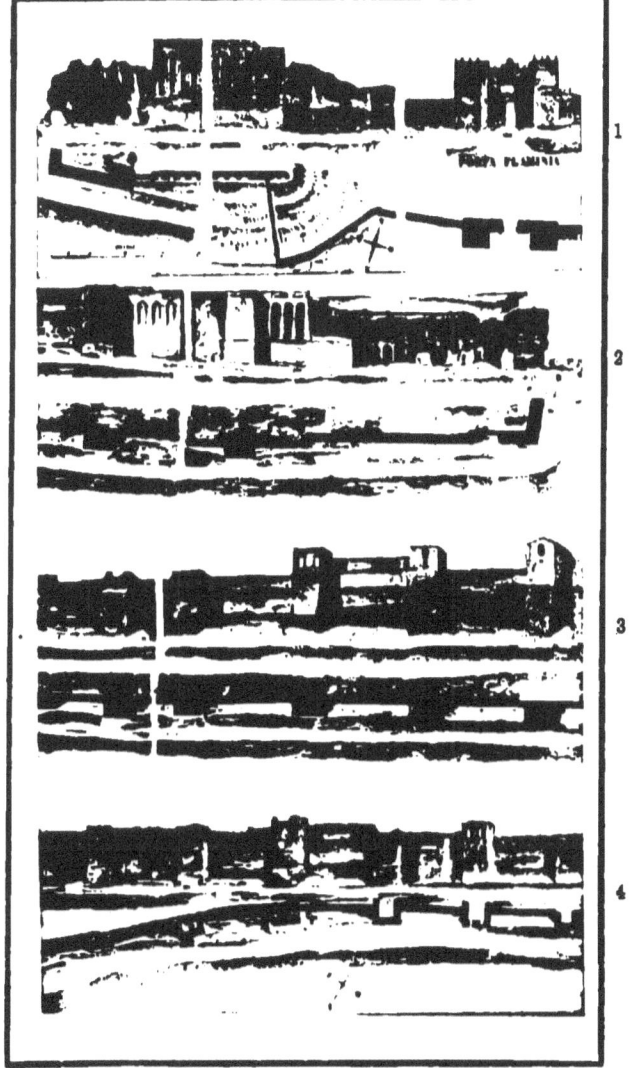

II.

5. PORTA PINCIANA. This is one of the most perfect gate-houses of the time of the Emperor Honorius, as restored by King Theodoric, that we have remaining; the stone-work of Honorius remains, the round brick towers belong to Theodoric, the square towers to the left are of the Wall of Aurelian. This gate is celebrated as the one to which Belisarius was refused admission by the Romans, who did not recognise him when returning from a sortie and reconnaissance. This gave rise to the story of his *begging at the gate* after a sortie; being pressed back by the Goths in pursuit, he probably *did* beg hard for recognition and to be admitted within the walls. In this part of the wall the corridor of Aurelian, or the sentinel's path, made in the thickness of the wall, is well shewn on the plan.

6. A continuation of the same wall, with repairs of the medieval period to the left.

7. PORTA SALARIA. This gate has been entirely destroyed, and a new one built in its place, since this photograph was taken. It was more picturesque than the new one, but was made out of old tombs, some of which were curious. An account of them will be found in the Chapter on Tombs.

8. Another part of the Wall of Aurelian, with its corridor, shewn on the plan, and with medieval and modern repairs.

WALLS AND GATES OF ROME. II.

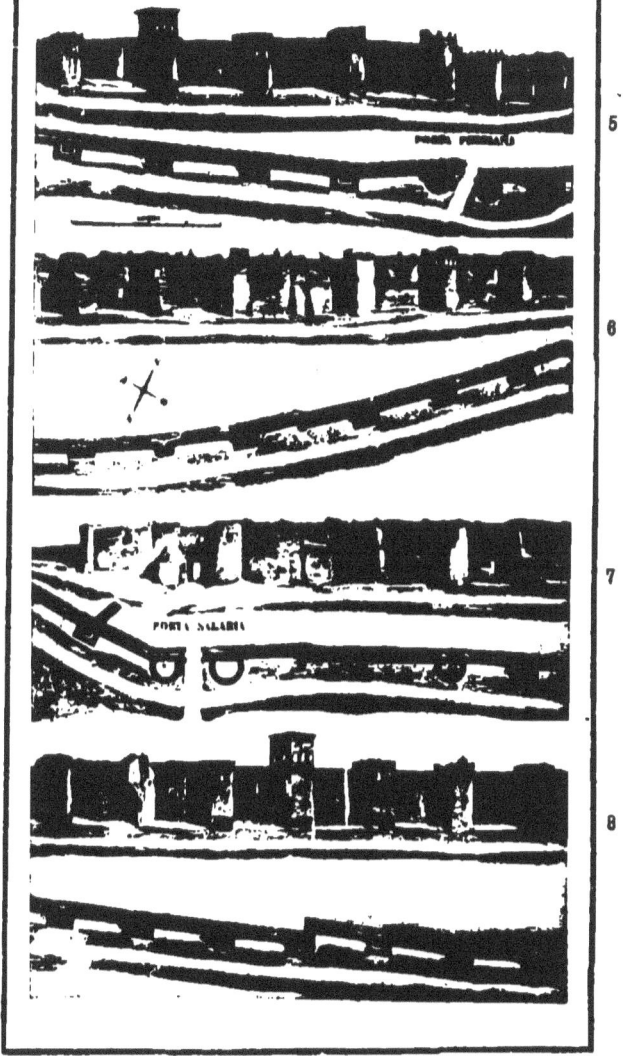

III.

9. PORTA NOMENTANA. Of this gate little more than ruins remain, and these are known to consist of old tombs; the modern Porta Pia is between the Porta Salaria and this; it is purposely omitted in our series because it is modern, and does not belong to archæology.

10. NORTH WALL OF THE PRÆTORIAN CAMP, with remains of the northern gate. A great part of this wall is original, of the time of Tiberius, with the beautiful brickwork of that period, built upon an older aqueduct, a branch of the Anio Vetus, which is faced with *Opus reticulatum* wherever the facing has not been destroyed. This was carried upon the old *mœnia* or earthwork of the camp, which is of the time of the Kings. The earth within the camp is from ten to fifteen feet above the level of the road on the outside. In the inner side of the wall, towards the south-west corner, are the old sleeping-places for the guards, shewn in the diagram towards the left.

11. The eastern wall of the Camp. It was dismantled by Constantine in consequence of a rebellion of the guards, and the present wall, after the repairs or rebuilding, is a piece of patchwork of various periods. The old round towers remain at the two ends.

12. The southern side of the Camp. In this part, when it was rebuilt, old materials were taken from a wall of the Kings, probably the one against the face of the *mœnia* in the great foss; the present road is made on the edge of that foss.

WALLS AND GATES OF ROME. III.

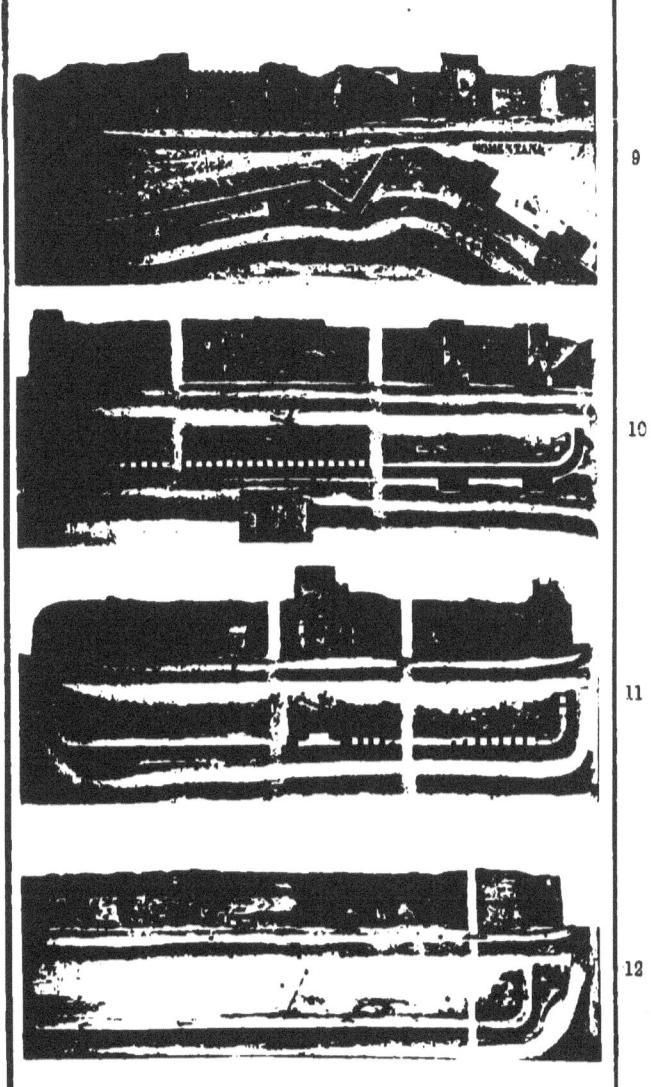

IV.

13. PORTA CHIUSA. This gate is called *chiusa*, or the closed gate, because it has long been closed, perhaps ever since the Camp was dismantled (it was an entrance into the Camp), and the antiquaries who gave the name to the gates in the seventeenth century could not agree about the name of this. The exterior face of the gate is of the time of Honorius, the interior partly of the time of the Republic, with several alterations. There is little doubt that it was on the original bridle road to Tibur or Tivoli. The present Porta Tiburtina is of the fifteenth century, and the modern carriage-road is made upon a bank across the great external foss.

14. To the right of this diagram will be seen a row of corbels, projecting boldly from the face of the wall, to carry a wooden gallery (such as were called *hourds*), a kind of scaffolding removable at pleasure. It is raised on the horizontal poles inserted in the holes left in the wall for that purpose (called put-log holes). The building incorporated in this part of the wall is popularly miscalled the House of Cicero, without any authority whatever for the name. It is in fact a great reservoir, or *castellum aquæ*, for the aqueduct called Tepula. Near this, to the left, is a postern gate, supposed to have been originally the Porta Prænestina, or bridle-road to Præneste or Palestrina, before the road was altered.

15. To the right of the diagram we see part of the aqueduct called Alexandrina, which carried water from the great reservoir at the highest level by the side of the Porta Maggiore, in which the water of the Claudia and the Anio Novus was united before it was distributed over Rome. The Alexandrina was a branch to carry water to the great Thermæ of the third century, on the eastern side of Rome, and to the Nymphæum, shewn by a coin to be of his time.

The Porta Maggiore is seen to the left of the diagram; it is the largest gate, and the principal entrance into Rome on the eastern side. It bears several different names, as mentioned in the text of the chapter on that subject.

16. Part of the Wall of the SESSORIUM with the AMPHITHEATRUM CASTRENSE, a fine piece of brickwork of the beginning of the second century, incorporated in the Wall of Aurelian. At the right-hand corner of the diagram is shewn a small plan of the *Vivarium*, in that part of the Sessorium, with the outer wall preserved, and the inner wall of the time of Aurelian built here in a straight line behind it. This enabled Belisarius to make the celebrated ambuscade which led to the entire defeat of the Gauls in a great panic.

WALLS AND GATES OF ROME. IV.

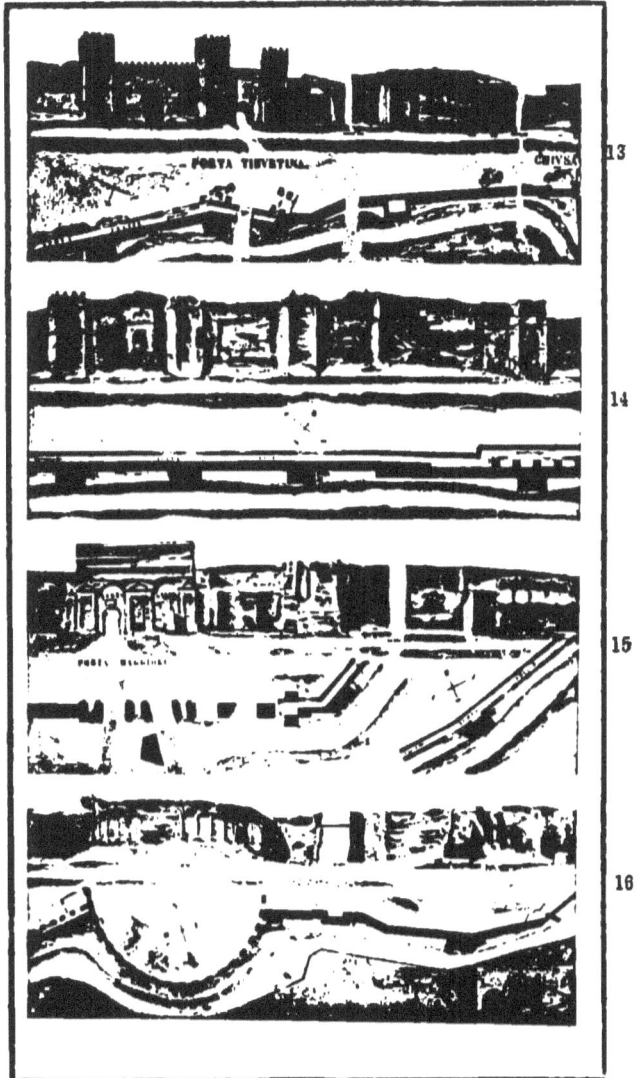

V.

17. PORTA ASINARIA and **PORTA S. GIOVANNI.** The Porta Asinaria is the old gate of the time of Aurelian, it is the only one of the gates of his wall that remains at all perfect. Most of them were rebuilt and fortified in the time of Honorius, rather more than a century after they were built, and restored by Theodoric another century afterwards. This gate stands at the old level of the foss-ways; the interior is almost buried by the filling-up of the foss-way. This gate appears also to have stood in the middle of an old fortress, the wings of which extend on both sides of it, though more perfect on the western side. Possibly this was part of the castle of the Asinii. The Porta S. Giovanni stands on the higher level of the new road of the seventeenth century, and belongs to that period.

18. PORTA LATERANENSIS. This gate is considered as a postern only, although the arch is of the usual size of a gate; it was one entrance to the old Lateran Palace, which here forms an angle projecting from the line of the Wall of Aurelian, in which it is incorporated.

19. PORTA METRONIA. This gate (long closed) is situated at the point where the Wall of Aurelian turns at a sharp angle to the south, to enclose the additional tongue of land added to the *pomærium* by Sylla. It stands upon a small bridge over that branch of the old river Almo that runs through Rome, the deep bed of which now conveys the water of the Marrana and Aqua Crabra united.

20. PORTA LATINA. This gate, which faces the north, has also long been closed; it is one of the most perfect of the gate-houses of Honorius. On each side are remains of a *castellum aquæ*, or reservoir, for an aqueduct, each on a different level, one for the Aqua Aurelia of Marcus Aurelius Commodus, the other for the Aqua Severiana of Septimius Severus, to supply their Thermæ just within this gate.

WALLS AND GATES OF ROME. V.

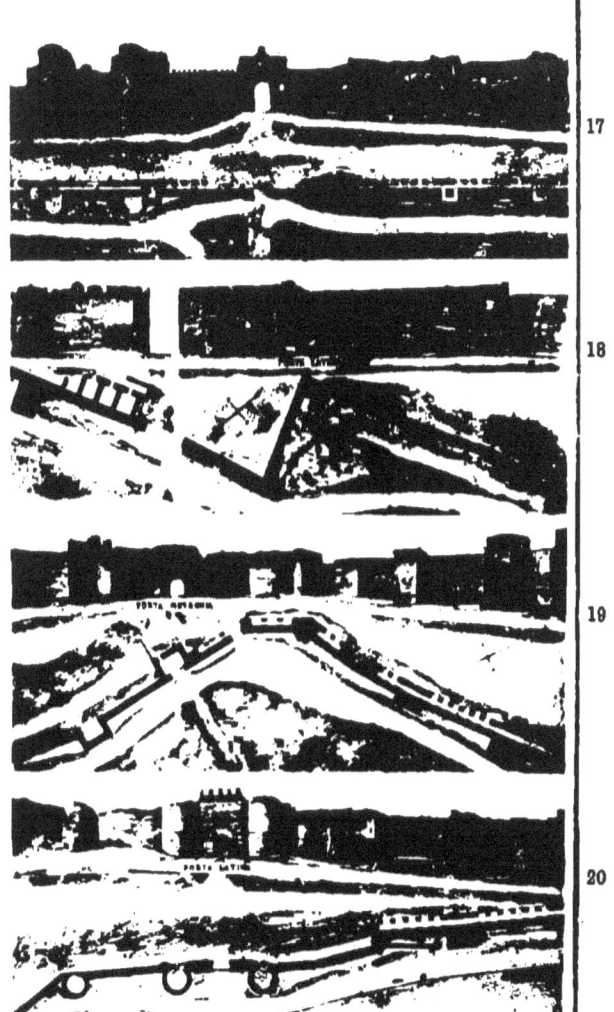

VI.

21. PORTA ARDEATINA. This gate is of the time of Nero, as is shewn by the construction; it stands at an angle in the Wall of Aurelian, and on the line of the old Via Ardeatina, or road from Ardea, which is older than the Via Appia.

PORTA S. SEBASTIANO, or APPIA. This is one of the gate-houses rebuilt by King Theodoric, as mentioned in his letters. The lower part of the towers is built of large blocks of marble, taken from the ruins of the temple of Mars, outside of this gate, the great southern entrance into Rome.

22. PORTA S. PAOLO, or OSTIENSIS. This gate, on the road to Ostia, is another of the gateway fortresses of King Theodoric, and the most perfect of them. The towers are of the Ravenna type. The inner gate, shewn on the plan, is of the time of Claudius, who was the first to build an outer wall to the Aventine, and thereby inclose a *pomœrium*. The pyramidal tomb of Caius Cestius is a conspicuous object at this gate, which stands in the old foss of the Aventine.

23. This view shews the angle of the wall when it arrives at the Tiber.

24. Shews the remains of the wall on the bank of the Tiber, with the Monte Testaccio behind it.

WALLS AND GATES OF ROME. VI.

VII.

25. THE JANICULUM, North side. In this view the scarped cliffs are visible, with the great foss at the foot, now a paved street, and the Wall of Aurelian built on the outer bank, and towers with mills made in them; other mills are also built up against the cliff.

26. The Janiculum, East side. Here again the cliffs are visible, and the zigzag road leading up to the summit. The church of S. Pietro in montorio (*monte aureo*) stands near the top, and is conspicuous on all sides.

27. The Janiculum, South side. This is a section through the hill, and shews the Porta S. Pancratio, the highest gate in Rome, on the summit to the left; the Aqua Paolo, or Alseatina-Trajana, a little lower down; and then the church on the edge of the cliff.

28. PLAN OF THE JANICULUM FORTRESS, with the suburb of the Trastevere below, extending to the Tiber.

WALLS AND GATES OF ROME.   VII.

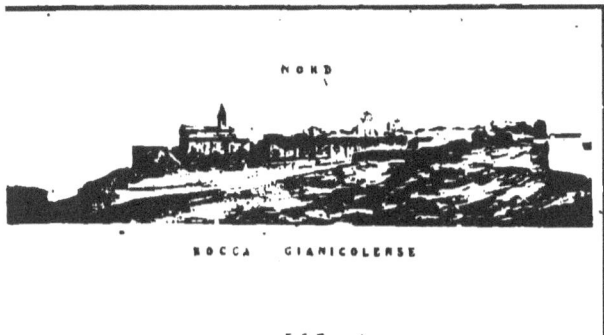

NORD

BOCCA GIANICOLENSE

EST

SVD

VIII.

29. THE JANICULUM, West side, shewing the cliff and the trench or foss, and the Wall of Aurelian built on the outer bank.

30. PORTA SETTIMIANA. This gate is in the valley, and near the Tiber, on the northern side of the hill. The towers of Aurelian in this part are unusually perfect.

31. PORTA S. SPIRITO, near the bank of the Tiber, in the LEONINE CITY, or the BORGO. The plan under it shews its exact position between the Vatican fortress and the Tiber.

32. The Castle of S. Angelo, originally the HADRIANUM, or the tomb-fortress of the Emperor Hadrian, with a plan of it. The passage on the top of the wall was made for the escape of the Pope in case of need, from the Vatican Palace to the Castle, the strongest fortress in Rome.

DESCRIPTION OF THE PHOTO-ENGRAVINGS

OF THE

WALLS AND GATES.

THE Series of Diagrams of the Walls and Gates, with plans under each portion from drawings by F. Cicconetti, has now been completed. It commences from the Porta Flaminia, near the Tiber on the north, passing down the eastern side of Rome to the Porta Ostiensis, and the Tiber at the south end of this great wall: then crossing the Tiber, and shewing what remains on the other side of the river, called the Trastevere, of the Wall of Aurelian on the Janiculum, the Hadrianum (now the castle of S. Angelo), and the Leonine City, called also the Borgo. As this line is thirteen miles long, it is obvious that there must be many breaks, at each of which the measurements are given of the part omitted; the omissions are of portions that are only repetitions, or are without interest. It is believed that this Series comprises all that is really interesting, and gives a general idea of this remarkable wall. The series of photographs, which now follows in the same order, supplies all the details as well as they can be seen on the spot, or sometimes better, for a photograph must always be obtained in a good light, which the passing traveller cannot always obtain, nor is it always easy to get at the inside of the wall, and this is often the most interesting portion. The great corridor of Aurelian for the sentinel's path, inside of his wall, is seldom understood from this cause.

Walls and Gates of Rome.

Plate I.

The Muro Torto. The celebrated distorted wall overhanging the foundations several feet, in consequence of their having given way, owing to the great pressure of the earth of the cliff behind the wall. The upper part was built upon the sloping wall in a series of semi-circular recesses or niches, after the settlement had taken place; the wall between the niches serves as buttresses to keep up the earth. This is at the eastern corner of the north end of the wall.

This very remarkable piece of early construction is well seen in the photograph; the overhanging of the wall is most evident, and explains why it has so long been considered dangerous, although there was no real danger. The skill of the builders in making that change of plan has removed the danger, and this interesting piece of architectural history will probably stand as many more centuries as it has already stood, if let alone. At the right-hand corner of the photograph, at the top, is seen a small piece of the hideous modern wall by which the architect of the Municipality intended to have concealed the whole of this curious ancient work. He has succeeded in doing so on the eastern side round the corner, but it is believed that the Muro Torto itself has been saved, at least for the present.

Niches near the Muro Torto. These are on the eastern side. They were evidently built after the settlement had taken place, and profiting by that lesson, the builders here erected the wall in a double series of niches from the ground; (this is now entirely concealed by the hideous modern wall, on the pretext that it was dangerous).

All this end of the Pincian Hill was the palace of Sylla.

WALLS OF ROME

NICHES NEAR MURO TORTO

Plate II.

Towers of Aurelian. These are some of the most perfect of the towers that remain, they are near the Porta Pinciana.

There are remains of many of these towers in a more or less perfect state; in two or three the old cornice and corbel-table remain, and a modern roof has been put on. The greater number of the towers that we have now remaining have been rebuilt in the time of the Popes at various periods, but chiefly in the fifteenth century.

Towers under the Villa Medici. The wall has been very much patched in this part, which now belongs to the French Academy; the original earth-works, on which the wall is built in many parts, are here clearly seen.

The portion of the plan given in the series of diagrams under each portion of the wall shews this more distinctly; in many parts the old earthworks, called the *mænia*, are distinctly visible, sometimes the rock itself on which the wall is built is seen. The wall under the Villa Medici has been so much patched at various periods, that no date can be now assigned to it. The tower has some approach to the rude work of the eighth century of Rome, but may be much later; rude work of this character may be of any period. This part of the wall is built against a cliff, the earth inside the wall is nearly level with the top of it.

WALLS OF ROME

TOWERS OF AURELIAN

TOWER UNDER VILLA MEDICI

WALLS AND GATES OF ROME.

PLATE III.

CASTELLUM AQUÆ TEPULÆ. EXTERIOR, NEAR THE PORTA DI S. LORENZO. This great reservoir of the Aqueducts stood on the bank before the Wall of Aurelian was built, and was incorporated into it. Along the front is seen a horizontal row of marble corbels to carry a wooden balcony or *hourd*, which was probably a passage for the *aquarii* or water-men, and might also serve for defence. Above are seen the windows of some chambers of a house, built over this great reservoir, as was frequently the case. It is popularly miscalled the "House of Cicero."

The abundant supply of water in the hot summer months of Rome was of so much importance, that it was very usual to erect some building over the great reservoirs of the aqueducts, and there is generally a reservoir of considerable size under each of the palaces.

INTERIOR, NEAR THE PORTA TIBURTINA, or di S. Lorenzo. This shews remains of another large reservoir near the other, probably for the Aqua Julia. This also stood on the bank before the Wall of Aurelian was built, and was of the time of Augustus; not being in the line of the wall it was not incorporated in that wall, but left within it, and was subsequently destroyed, and a road made through it. There is no reason to suppose that the aqueducts were destroyed by the engineers of Aurelian; they were used as part of the wall when they came in the line of it, but when within it were probably let alone. Those on the outside of the line (of which there are many remains) were probably destroyed, as they would have interfered with the defence.

CASTELLUM AQUAE TEPULAE

INTERIOR NEAR P.ª TIBURTINA

Walls and Gates of Rome.

Plate IV.

POSTERN IN THE WALL near the Porta S. Lorenzo, supposed to have been a postern on the old bridle-road to Collatia and Præneste, before the carriage-road was made. Two or three bridle-roads were often merged in one carriage-road, after the use of carriages within the walls was permitted. This was not until the time of the Emperors. During the whole long period of the Republic the use of wheeled carriages within the walls of Rome was forbidden. Gentlemen rode on horseback, and ladies were carried in palanquins.

The old bridle-roads seem to have gone straight from the town whose name each road bore, not only up to the *mœnia*, but crossing the great foss, and over the bank, still in a straight line, to the gate in the inner wall of Servius Tullius. Two or three roads generally meet at each of these inner gates, but the carriage-roads of the time of the early Empire met at the outer gates. For instance, the Via Prenestina, or road from Præneste, and the Via Labicana, or road from Labicum, meet at the Porta Maggiore. The old bridle-roads of the time of the Kings and of the Republic can generally be traced, and followed each in straight lines to within about half a mile of the present wall, originally the outer wall: near Rome they are intercepted by modern gardens, and cannot be followed.

PART OF THE WALL AND AQUEDUCT combined, near the Porta Maggiore. The aqueducts had been carried on the high bank here before the time of Aurelian, and were incorporated in his wall for about a mile, from the Porta Maggiore to the Prætorian Camp. This portion belonged to the Aqua Alexandrina, and extended only as far as the building called Minerva Medica, which was a nymphæum belonging to the great thermæ of the third century on the eastern side of Rome, to which this branch-aqueduct conveyed the water.

Just beyond the point shewn in the photograph the arcade in the wall ceases, immediately opposite to the great *castellum aquæ*, ot which there are remains between the wall and the Nymphæum called Minerva Medica. This aqueduct evidently led from the great reservoir at the Porta Maggiore to the thermæ of the third century within the wall at that point.

WALLS OF ROME

POSTERN IN WALL

WALL AND AQUEDUCT

PLATE V.

PORTA MAGGIORE, side view, shewing the aqueducts over it. These are the Claudia, and the Anio Novus at one of the angles of that aqueduct-arcade; the Marcia, Tepula, and Julia passed under them through the wall a little to the right of this view.

PORTA MAGGIORE, front view, a celebrated typical example of Rustic work; it is of the time of the Emperor Claudius; to the right is the Baker's Tomb between two roads, which met at that gate. The ground has been raised about ten feet since this gate and tomb were built, which injures the proportions of them.

The effigies of the baker and his wife ought to be restored to the place that they originally occupied at the end of the tomb, visible from both the roads. These effigies were found in 1833 among the rubbish with which the round tower of Honorius had been filled. They are now built up in a wall on the opposite side of the road. The tomb itself had been found in one of the towers or bastions of the gate, and it was probably not observed at the time that they evidently came from the end of this tomb. The *specus* or conduit of the aqueduct was carried over the gate as was necessary, and the usual form of the *specus* of these two aqueducts is visible in this view; and the gateway, with this portion of the *specus*, is of the time of Claudius, when the aqueduct was made. There are inscriptions upon it giving the measurements from the sources to this point, shewing clearly that this was considered as the entrance into ROME, though not into the CITY.

WALLS AND GATES

PORTA MAGGIORE, SIDE VIEW

PORTA MAGGIORE, FRONT VIEW

PLATE VI.

PORTA LATERANENSIS. This is considered a postern only, although the arch shews that it was of considerable size, and some excavations made down to the base of it in 1870 shew there were tombs outside of it, as was usual at the principal gates. It was the external entrance to the great Lateran Palace of Plautius Lateranus.

The existence of this gate is little known, because it is concealed by the earth thrown up against it to make a snug little vineyard in the angle formed by the projection of the Lateran Palace from the line of the Wall of Aurelian. The architect of the wall respected the old palace, and did not disturb it. The tombs found in the excavation seem to shew that it was a public gate, and not merely a postern. The road from it can be traced across the meadows and over two bridges to the old Via Latina.

PORTA ASINARIA. This is the most perfect of the gates of Aurelian; it has remains of two wings to it, and was a gatehouse of considerable importance, and was probably the entrance to the palace of the great family of the Asinii. It stands on the low level of the bridle-roads, or the foss-way, and was closed in the sixteenth century, when a new carriage-road was made on the high level nearly twenty feet above the old road. The entrance is closed, and in the interior it has earth piled up against it higher than the top of the arch. The Porta San Giovanni is on the high level of the modern road by the side of it.

WALLS AND GATES

PORTA LATERANENSIS

PORTA ASINARIA

PLATE VII.

PORTA APPIA, now called di San Sebastiano, exterior and interior. This fine gate-house is of several periods, as it has been rebuilt more than once; the upper part of the towers, round outside and flat inside, are of the time of King Theodoric, c. A.D. 500. The outer casing below is also of his time; this lower part is faced with large blocks of marble, evidently used again from a previous building, supposed to have been the temple of Mars, which stood just outside of this gate,—the great southern gate of Rome in the outer wall. The upper part of the towers is of brickwork of the Ravenna type. In the interior the arch of Drusus is seen standing in front of the gate on the Via Appia, which is here a foss-way; the earth on each side is level with the top of the arch, and of the walls by the side of the road, as is seen by the trees growing on it.

This great southern gate of the City of the third century is just a mile from the Porta Capena, which had long been the great southern gate of the CITY OF ROME of the time of the Kings, and continued to be so until the time of Aurelian. For the last two or three centuries these two gates have been confounded together by the local antiquaries, according to what are called the Roman traditions; this mistake was natural, because it was known that an aqueduct was carried over the Porta Capena, and an aqueduct was visible over the Arch of Drusus, just within this entrance gate; but that aqueduct is of the third century, and carried the Aqua Antoniana for the supply of the great Thermæ of the Antonines, now called of Caracalla, whereas over the Porta Capena passed the aqueduct of Trajan, as is seen by the existing remains, and that was made over the earlier aqueducts, the Appia and the Marcia. That the Porta Appia was made in the outer *mœnia* is evident, because the first Regio of Augustus was precisely the space, a mile long, between these two gates. This was called after the Porta Capena, which was the entrance from it into THE CITY, whilst the Porta Appia was the entrance into Rome as distinct from THE CITY. That part of the Wall of Aurelian in which the Porta Appia stands is the most perfect. The arcade or corridor within the wall, for the sentinel's path, is perfect on both sides of this gate for the space of about half-a-mile.

PORTA APPIA, EXTERIOR

PORTA APPIA, INTERIOR

WALLS AND GATES OF ROME.

PLATE IX.

PORTA S. LORENZO, interior, with aqueducts. This is an important view, in many respects it shews a great deal of history. On the left is a modern house, in the wall of which is seen one pier of the inner arch of the Barbican of the gate of the time of Honorius. This being the gate in the outer wall on the road to Tibur or Tivoli, was a very important one, and was strongly fortified. The remainder of this arch was destroyed by order of the Pontifical Government in 1870, in order to use the old travertine for a base to the marble column to be erected on the Janiculum, to commemorate the Council at which the doctrine of Infallibility was to be promulgated. The column has not been erected, and the stones of this arch were lying on the ground on the platform in front of the church of S. Pietro in Montorio in 1873. The arch in the centre of this view is of the time of Augustus, and has inscriptions upon it recording his restoration of the aqueducts, which were carried over it — the Marcia, Tepula, and Julia. Remains of these aqueducts are visible in the wall on the right of the gate. The Marcia is built of squared stones, five feet high and two wide, so that a man could walk in it. Upon this are remains of the Tepula, built of brick. The *specus* of this is rather higher and narrower than that of the Marcia, and it has a pointed head, whereas that of the Marcia is flat. Of the Aqua Julia, above the Tepula, the remains are here very small. A little further to the right of this view a *castellum aquæ*, or reservoir of the Aqua Felice is visible in the wall. Beyond this, more to the right, are remains of the vault of an old reservoir, probably of the Julia, at a lower level than the Felice; the remains of the vault are seen in a straight black line on the engraving. This reservoir has long been destroyed, and the present modern road inside the wall runs through it. The archway of Augustus is buried up to the springing of the arch, by the filling-up of the foss-way on which it stood; the whole of the jambs or piers of the arch are buried; the present level of the road is the natural level of the ground, from twelve to fifteen feet above the level of the old foss-way. The filling-up must have been made between the time of Augustus, A.D. 10, and that of Honorius, A.D. 400, because the jambs of the arch of Honorius stand on the present level of the ground, which is the same now that it was then. The outer arch of Honorius, at the other end of the Barbican, remains, and is shewn in the plate on the exterior of the gate. The arch of Augustus was in the middle, between these two gates of Honorius.

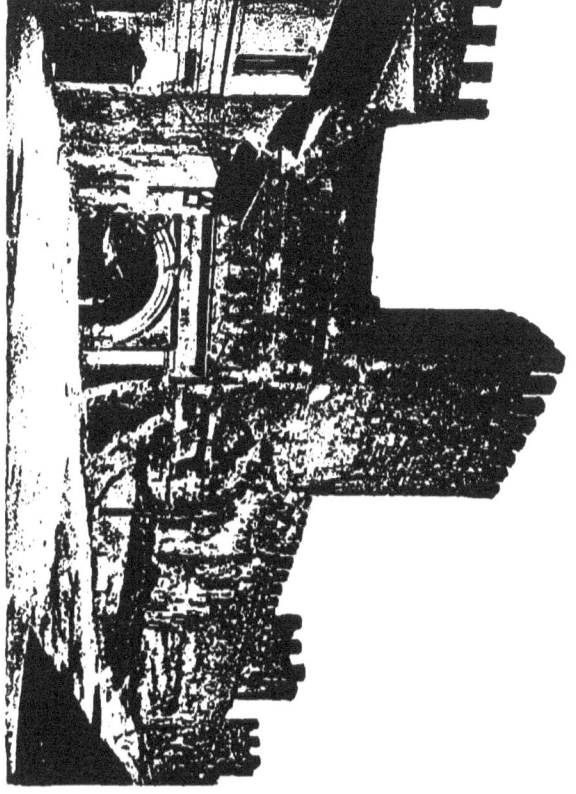

PORTA S. LORENZO INTERIOR WITH AQUEDUCTS.

WALLS AND GATES OF ROME.

WALLS AND GATES OF ROME.

PLATE X.

CORRIDOR OF AURELIAN, FROM THE PORTA ARDEATINA TO THE PORTA APPIA, or di S. Sebastiano. This is one of the most perfect parts of the corridor for the sentinels in the Wall of Aurelian. There are other parts equally perfect, especially that between the Porta Appia and the Porta Latina. This corridor is not generally understood by the visitors to Rome, and is often mistaken for an aqueduct, to which at first sight it bears considerable resemblance at a certain distance; but instead of this arcade carrying the *specus* of the aqueduct across the country, it only carries the *allure* or sentinels' path on the top of the wall behind the parapet from one tower to another, and there were always steps in each tower to ascend from the path below under the arcade to that above. In times of peace, the sentinels only passed from one tower to another in the corridor under shelter; in times of war, they could immediately man the wall upon the *allure* when that was necessary. Another very perfect part of this corridor remains between the Porta di S. Giovanni and the Church of S. Croce in Gerusalemme, and as that is by the side of a road much frequented, it is more often seen than those in the vineyards, and it is continually mistaken for an aqueduct by visitors, often indeed by those who have been long resident in Rome. This corridor is said to be the finest thing of the kind that exists anywhere; it was frequently imitated in the fortifications of the Middle Ages, especially in Aquitaine, as in Avignon, the wall of the Popes round the town; but the imitation, though a fine thing of its kind, is by no means equal to the original.

CORRIDOR OF AURELIAN FROM PORTA APDEATINA TO PORTA APPIA.

WALLS AND GATES OF ROME.

PLATE XI.

INTERIOR OF THE CORRIDOR, WITH A PAINTING OF THE MADONNA, said to be of the sixth century, and probably the work of some of the Greek soldiers from Byzantium, serving under Belisarius during the time of the great siege by the Goths, recorded by Procopius, one of the officers of that Greek corps. The painting is a very remarkable one, and agrees with the art of that period. A further account of it will be found in the Chapter on Fresco Painting. This curious old painting had been entirely overlooked, and is not mentioned by any author. I discovered it by mere accident in 1870, in making out the history of the Walls of Rome. I had frequently passed under it without seeing it, because I had usually gone the opposite way, and saw only the back of the lath and plaster partition on which it is painted. The painting is on the west side, and I had usually passed from east to west in this part, and had gone out by a different way. Many others have no doubt done the same. At first I could not believe that it was of so early a period, but several independent witnesses, better acquainted than myself with the history of the art, have assured me that it is so; they point out the foliage painted on the brick arch as peculiar, and certainly early, and of whatever date that is, the head is certainly of the same date.

WALLS OF ROME.

MADONNA CENT. VI IN THE CORRIDOR OF AURELIAN NEAR THE PORTA APPIA.

XII

DESCRIPTION OF THE PLATES.

CONSTRUCTION OF WALLS.

CONSTRUCTION OF WALLS.

PLATE I.

OPUS QUADRATUM.

1. FIRST PERIOD. ROMULUS (?). This construction is found only on the Palatine Hill, on three sides of *Roma Quadrata*, and in the foundations of the Temple of Jupiter Feretrius, built in the year iv. of Rome, in the *arx* or Capitol of Romulus, and in the steps of Cacus (?) leading up to it.

The walls of this period are distinguished by the width of the vertical joints, called *wide-jointed masonry*, and the rude construction. The probable date of it is from B.C. 753 to 720, or the first thirty years of Rome, *Annis Urbis Conditæ* (A.U.C.) 1—33.

2. SECOND PERIOD. B.C. 713, A.U.C. 39, to A.U.C. 177, B.C. 576. THE TABULARIUM. In this the vertical joints are closely fitted together, it is what is called *fine-jointed masonry*. It is part of the great building called the Capitolium, erected when the two hills were made into one City, and enclosed in one wall. This great building contained all the public offices necessary for the new City, the future progress of which was anticipated. The stones are larger than those on the Palatine, but this may be only because they are from a different quarry. The construction of the *Ærarium* under the Tabularium is the same, but part of it has been faced with small square stones, probably by King Theodoric, who repaired many of the ancient buildings of Rome.

CONSTRUCTION. OPUS QUADRATUM

FIRST PERIOD B C 753-720 ROMULUS?

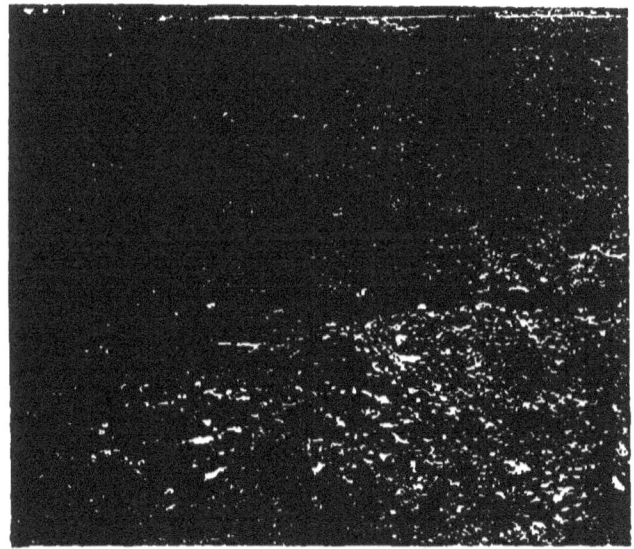

TABULARIUM B C 713. A U C. 39

PLATE II.

1. MAMERTINE PRISON. This piece of the wall is taken at an angle where there is a junction, and a slight change in the construction (as may be seen in the photograph), the joints not being in the same level, and the stones not from the same quarry. It was a great work, and was not all built at once. The original part was built by King Ancus Martius, an addition was made to it by Servius Tullius, which was called the Robur Tullianum. This plate shews the junction of the two walls.

2. WALL OF THE LATINS ON THE AVENTINE. This is part of a section of the wall, which is here twelve feet thick and fifty feet high, built against the cliff to support it. The wide joints between the stones would seem at first sight to indicate the time of Romulus, but on the surface of the wall the stones are closely fitted together, and it belongs to the second period. In the interior of the wall the work was less carefully done, and the wide joints are left. They seem to shew that no mortar was used originally, although on the surface the joints appear to have been pointed with mortar at some later period. This great wall stands upon a ledge of the tufa rock cut away to a level surface, which formed a great wide and deep foss on the outside of the wall.

CONSTRUCTION. OPUS QUADRATUM

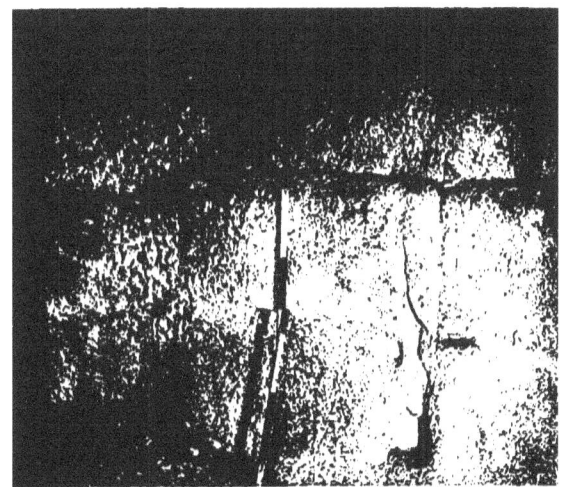

MAMERTINE PRISON. B.C. 639. A.U.C. 114

WALL OF THE AVENTINE. B.C. 639. A.U.C. 114

CONSTRUCTION OF WALLS.

PLATE III.

1. This is part of the section of the second Wall of Rome, the great wall that enclosed the two hills into one City; it is fifty feet high and twelve feet thick. In the lower part is seen a portion of another wall built of travertine, (the different nature of this limestone from the tufa is very visible in the photograph). This wall of travertine limestone was the partition wall between the Forum of Augustus and the Forum Transitorium of Nerva. The great wall was used for the eastern boundary of the Forum of Augustus, but was built long before his time, and was made use of, because it stood there ready for use, and it would not pay to remove it, each stone being a ton weight. It was afterwards used as the western wall of the castle of the Conti, or Counts of Anagni.

2. Another part of the wall of the great Prison of the Kings; here the joints are very fine, and are continued at the same level, and the stones are of the usual dimensions, each four feet long and two feet thick, as may be seen in the photograph by the measure placed against the wall. Another wall of this great prison is of the time of Servius Tullius, distinguished by the holes at the edges of the stones, from which the iron clamps have fallen out, which were not used before his time. This wall also has a straight vertical joint between it and the other earlier wall against which it abuts. This must have been one of the walls of the Robur Tullianum.

CONSTRUCTION. OPUS QUADRATUM

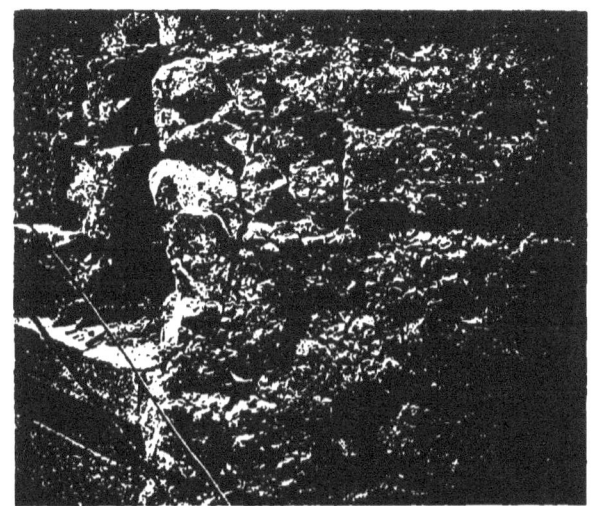

WALL IN THE FORUM OF AUGUSTUS. B. C. 720-700?

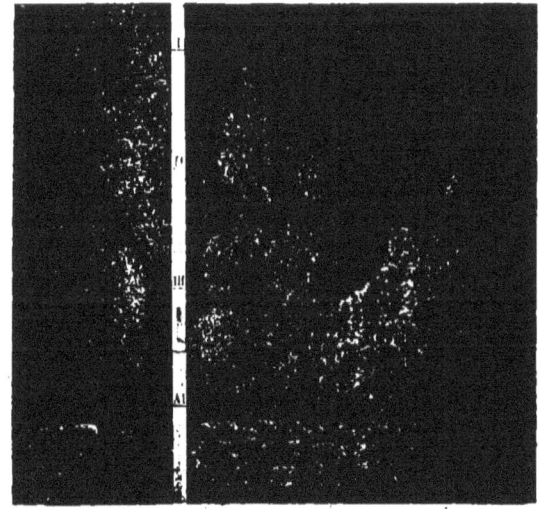

MAMERTINE PRISON B.C. 639. A.U.C. 114

PLATE IV.

1. WALL UNDER S. ANASTASIA, *c.* A.U.C. 39, B.C. 714. There are remains of two square massive towers at the foot of the Palatine, on the western side, now under the church, and this photograph is taken at an angle of one of them. The construction is of the second period (*fine-jointed masonry*), quite distinct from the *wide-jointed masonry* of *Roma Quadrata*. These towers (the lower part of which only remains) are usually called the *Pulvinarium* (or cushioned gallery) of the Circus Maximus. They may have been used for that purpose, being conveniently situated for the object, but it is not at all probable that such work would be built for that purpose. They evidently belong to the *Second Wall of Rome*, to enclose the two hills in one City, another part of which remains behind the houses at the foot of the Palatine Hill (now in the Via dei Cerchi), a hundred yards to the south of these towers.

2. WALL OF SERVIUS TULLIUS, A.U.C. 189, B.C. 564. This is part of the wall that faced the great *agger*, in that part that was destroyed to enlarge the railway station in 1871, and the wrought-iron clamps were found in the middle of the wall, where they could not fall out, as they had done on the outside of the wall, and left the holes (here seen) at the edges of the stones. The photograph shews also the junction of one of the towers with the wall, and it has slight remains of painting of the time of the early Empire upon it, shewing that a house had been built up against it, in the line of the street made in the foss, the pavement of which was also found five yards below the surface.

WALL UNDER S. ANASTASIA. B. C. 713. A. U. C. 39

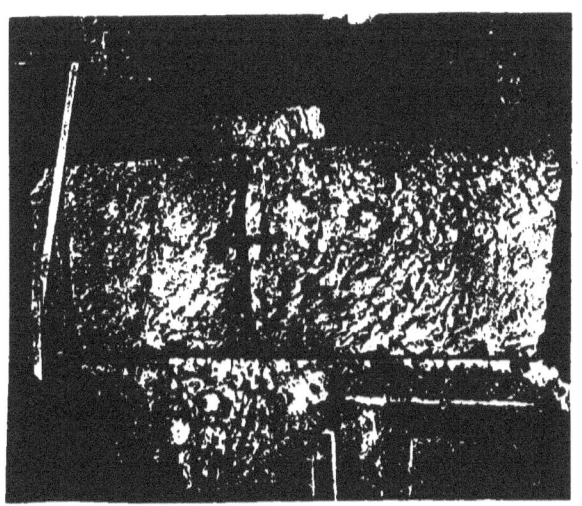

WALL OF SERVIUS TULLIUS. B. C. 189. A. U. C. 564

PLATE V.

CONCRETE. FARTURA.

1. FORT ON THE AVENTINE, B.C. 300 (?). This ancient fort is under S. Sabba, the walls are built of concrete in layers, and have rather the appearance of having been cast in boxes, as is now done in the pier at Dover, and supposed to be a new invention. But the appearance is perhaps deceptive, we can only be certain that it was made in layers (in the same manner as is done by Mr. Tall in his new patent concrete walls). This wall was originally faced with the squared stones or *Opus quadratum*, some of which remain at the foot of the wall, about ten feet underground; parts of them remaining *in situ* were shewn in the excavations of 1871.

2. VILLA OF HADRIAN AT TIVOLI, A.D. 120. This is part of the core of the wall, and was faced with the panelling of bricks and reticulated-work used in his time; but the core of the walls of the time of the Empire was generally of concrete only, and the ornamental construction was on the surface.

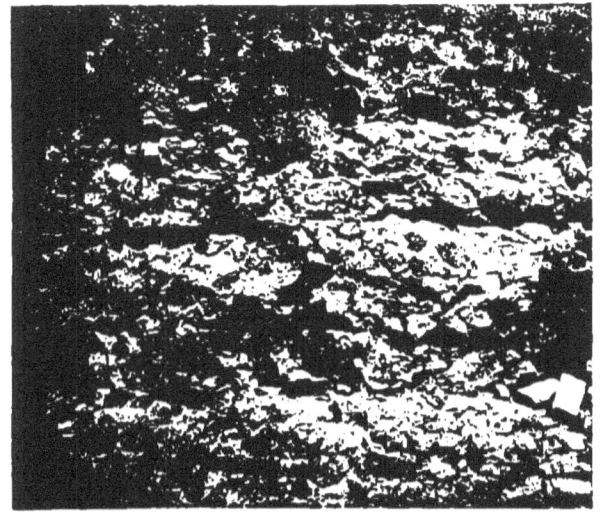

FORT ON THE AVENTINE B. C. 300?

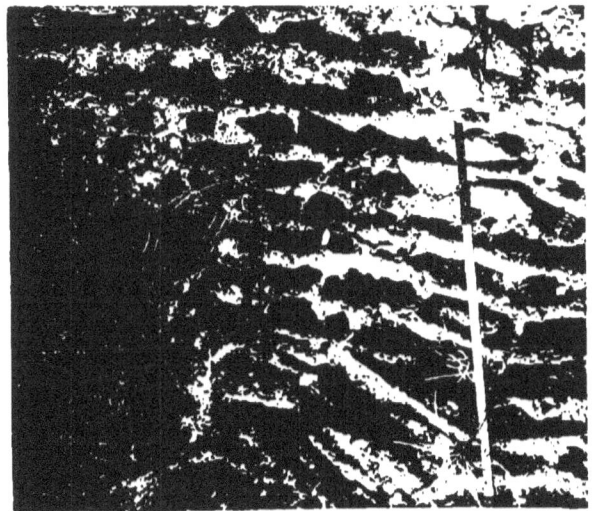

VILLA OF HADRIAN AT TIVOLI

PLATE VI.

OPUS INCERTUM.

1. IRREGULAR WORK. These names apply to the surface only. The ornamental construction was intended to be seen; the real construction in most cases is a mass of concrete or rubble, called *fartura* in Latin, and *a sacco* in Italian. This *Opus incertum* is an earlier stage of the *Opus reticulatum*; it is generally characteristic of the time of the Republic, as the *reticulatum* is of the time of the Early Empire. The larger blocks of tufa, looking at first sight like large bricks, were continued in use as late as the time of Tiberius, but are then used with *Opus reticulatum* of the regular kind.

2. HOUSE ON THE VIMINAL HILL. The situation is against the cliff, near the remains of the Lavacrum of Agrippina (destroyed in 1872), and opposite to the church of S. Vitale, which is at the foot of the Quirinal. The new grand street of modern Rome, called the Via Nazionale, now passes between these two hills upon a high embankment. The house has not yet been identified, but is of the time of Sylla. The oblong blocks of tufa have even more of the appearance of large bricks than in the Emporium; the wall that is faced in that manner is hollow, a space of two feet wide being left in it, probably to keep the rooms dry, as the moisture of the earth behind would penetrate through a solid wall.

CONSTRUCTION. OPUS INCERTUM

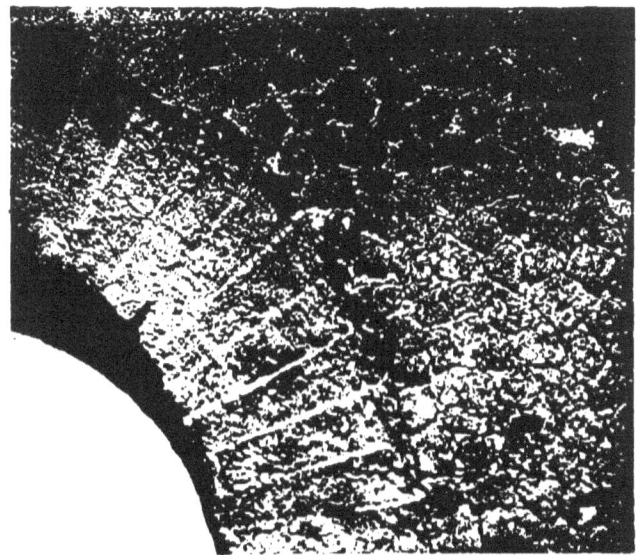

EMPORIUM B C 175

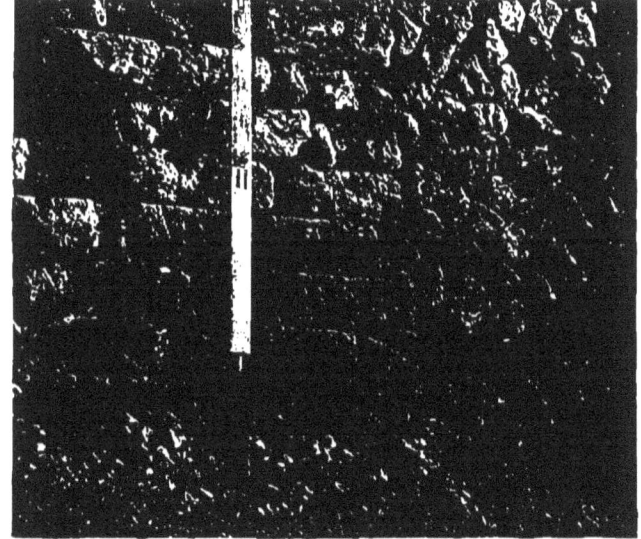

PLATE VII.

OPUS RETICULATUM.

1. MURO TORTO, B.C. 80 (?). This is a valuable example of the early kind of reticulated-work, and bears out the idea of a net thrown over the wall. There is no mortar visible, although the points of the wedges of the small diamond-shaped blocks are inserted in the mortar of the rubble-work behind before it had set, or probably grouted in with lime-grouting in a fluid state, which binds the whole wall together in a solid mass, the surface made smooth in this manner. This enabled the wall to hold together when the foundations gave way, and it hangs over several feet.

2. MAUSOLEUM OF AUGUSTUS. This is the example of reticulated-work usually referred to as the historical type, as there can be no doubt about the date of it. In this the mortar is plainly visible, which is considered as one of the distinctions between the work of the Empire and that of the Republic; but the distinctions between the different varieties of *Opus reticulatum* are hardly clear enough to be generally attended to. The fact is sufficient in most cases, that this mode of facing a wall was in use throughout the first century; beginning a little before it, and continuing a short time after it.

CONSTRUCTION. OPUS RETICULATUM

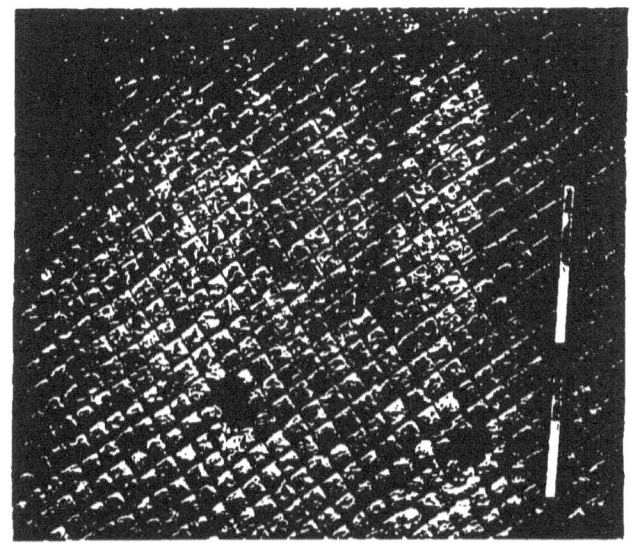

MURO TORTO. B. C 80?

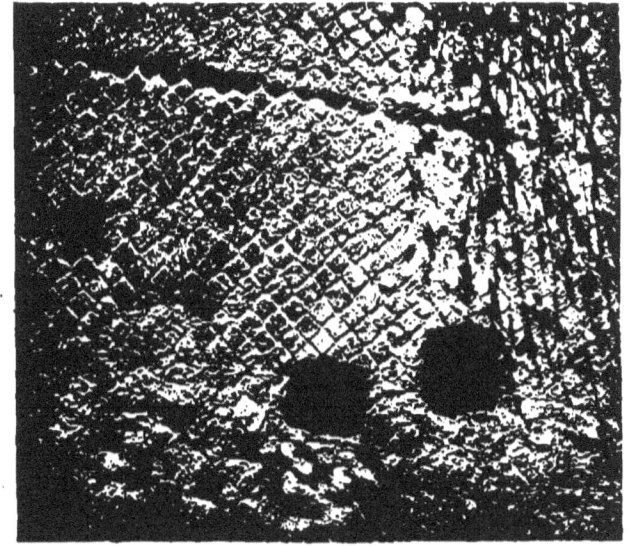

MAUSOLEUM OF AUGUSTUS. B.C. 28

PLATE VIII.

OPUS RETICULATUM ET LATERITIUM.

1. HOUSE OF NERO. This combination of the reticulated-work with brickwork generally indicates rather later date than the reticulated-work separately. This mixture begins as early as the time of Nero, but at that time the bricks are extremely thin, and there is scarcely any mortar between them. The small diamond-shaped wedges of the reticulated-work are larger than they are at an earlier period, but the joints are very fine, almost as fine as in the brickwork.

2. VILLA OF HADRIAN AT TIVOLI. In the time of Hadrian, the early part of the second century, the wedges are of about the same size, but the mortar between them is much thicker than at the earlier period. The bricks are also much thicker, and have much more mortar between them, indicating a later date; after the time of Hadrian there are no genuine examples of reticulated-work.

This is a good historical type of the period, as there can be no doubt about the date of it. Precisely the same construction occurs on the Palatine Hill, at the north-east corner, in the partition walls of the chambers. That part of the palaces of the Cæsars must therefore be of the time of Hadrian. At the north-west corner there are walls of the same character and period in the guard-chambers.

CONSTRUCTION. RETICULATUM ET LATERIT.

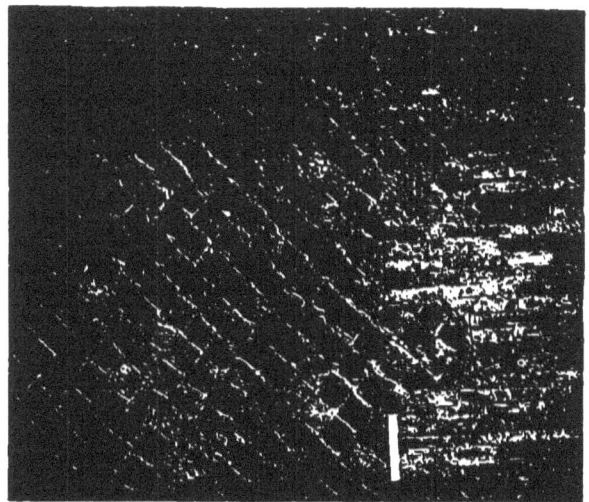

HOUSE OF NERO A D 60

VILLA OF HADRIAN AT TIVOLI A D 120

PLATE IX.
TRAVERTINE.

1. MAMERTINE PRISON, TIBERIUS, A.D. 22. The upper part of the great prison of the Kings was rebuilt in the time of Tiberius, and the exact date is recorded by an inscription on that part of it which is called the Prison of S. Peter. Construction of the same period is found in the Vicolo del Ghettarello, where the other part is situated; in both parts the walls of the underground chambers are of tufa of the time of the Kings. In the part before us the stones of the arcade have been taken from the Tullianum, or the part added by Servius Tullius, and have been used again, as may be seen by the holes at the edges of those which do not fit; when a wall of that period has not been rebuilt, there are the corresponding holes in the two stones which have been held together by an iron clamp. In the arcade the springing stones are of travertine, this being the point on which the arches rest, as the most essential part of the construction; the arches and superstructure are of old tufa stones used again.

2. TEMPLE OF ANTONINUS AND FAUSTINA, FROM THE CELLA. This may be called *Opus quadratum*, but the difference of the material marks the distinction between this and the Walls of the Kings. Travertine was not used until near the time of the Empire.

CONSTRUCTION. TRAVERTINE

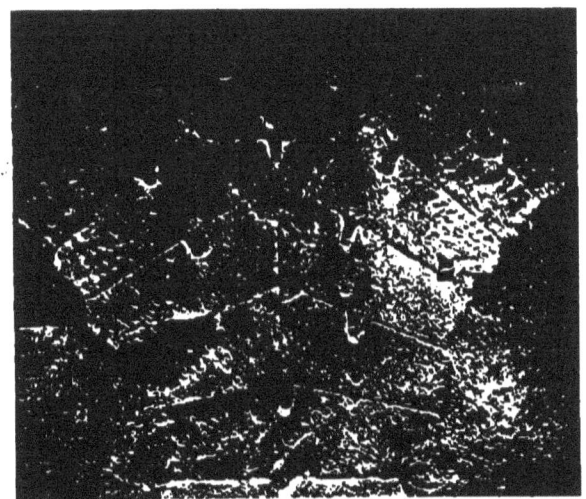

MAMERTINE PRISON - TIBERIUS A.D. 22

TEMPLE OF FAUSTINA A.D. 161

PLATE X.

1. TRAVERTINE. From the tomb of Cæcilia Metella, B.C. 103, two miles from Rome. This is the earliest example known of the use of travertine, and it is merely a veneer over a rubble wall of enormous thickness. The open cell for the sarcophagus in the centre is comparatively small, considering the enormous size of the mausoleum as a whole. The eye readily distinguishes travertine with its fine joints from the old tufa walls, and the plates of travertine are not nearly so large as the blocks of tufa.

There is some doubt as to the date of this tomb, the one here given, is, that generally considered as correct by the Roman antiquaries; but others think B.C. 50 more probable. Cecilia Metella was a family name, and we know of at least two of that name; this one was married to Crassus, but that also is a family name, and in either case it may be of one or the other generation. Crassus, who was Triumvir with Julius Cæsar and Mark Antony, B.C. 50, was called the rich Crassus, and this tomb has evidently been built for a wealthy family.

2. TEMPLE OF FORTUNA, A.D. 10. The temple is of two periods and two building materials. The porticus or portico is of travertine, and has a richly-sculptured cornice; the intervals between the columns are filled up with medieval brick wall, with a stone doorway of the same period. But the cella to which the portico had originally belonged is in some parts of tufa, and the cornice is quite plain. The portion here given belongs to the oldest part, and the columns are cut on the face of the blocks, not worked as separate detached columns placed against the walls. The exact date of the early part is doubtful, but B.C. 90 is the most likely one. It is probably one of the earliest examples of fluted Ionic columns in Rome.

CONSTRUCTION. TRAVERTINE

TOMB OF CAECILIA METELLA, B.C. 103

TEMPLE OF FORTUNA, A.D. 10

PLATE XI.

Opus Lateritium, Brickwork.

1. House of Nero on the Esquiline, A.D. 60. This belongs to the best period of brickwork in Rome, or anywhere; in the arches, where the best bricks are used, nine or ten to the foot can be counted, mortar included; this example is a tympanum over a doorway, and the intermediate part between the flat brick lintel and the arch over it, appears to be a filling-up of a later time. It was all covered over with plaster, and painted.

2. Arches of Nero on the Cœlian, belonging to his Aqueduct. As this was intended to be seen, and not plastered over, the brickwork is more carefully finished; the third arch of construction under the two others is of a later period. There were originally two only. This example is usually cited, as *the historical type* of the brickwork of the middle of the first century, the best period. The bricks themselves are remarkably hard and well-made, and there is scarcely any mortar between them.

CONSTRUCTION. OPUS LATERITIUM

HOUSE OF NERO. A.D. 60

ARCHES OF NERO ON THE COELIAN A.D. 60

PLATE XII.

OPUS LATERITIUM, BRICKWORK.

1. AMPHITHEATRUM CASTRENSE, A.D. 135. This is a remarkably fine example of the brickwork of the second period, not quite so good as the first, but still exceedingly good. All the mouldings and the foliage of the capitals are also of brick, worked by hand, not cast in a mould, belonging to the class called *terra cotta*. In this the bricks are thicker than in the best period, and are only eight to the foot, not ten.

2. THERMÆ OF THE ANTONINES, usually called after the last of them, ANTONINUS CARACALLA, in whose time they were nearly completed and were opened; but the porticus in front of them was then unfinished, and was completed by Heliogabalus, with a bath-chamber under each of the arches of the arcade. In this great building the brickwork, though still very good, is not so good as before, and there are only six bricks to the foot, there being much more mortar between them.

The *porticus* between the main building and the Via Appia appears to have been a double arcade one over the other; the lower story only remains, and that in ruins, but the top is evidently incomplete, and portions of the upper arches remain.

The *porticus* of the Golden House of Nero, which was a mile long, appears to have been a double arcade of the same kind, of which there are remains at intervals along the line. In that part which is against the western cliff of the Velia, the upper part of the double arcade is perfect, the lower part has been altered or destroyed. The Velia was always reckoned as part of the Palatine, and there is no brickwork of the time of Nero in any other part.

CONSTRUCTION. OPUS LATERITIUM

AMPHITHEATRUM CASTRENSE. A.D. 135

THERMAE OF CARACALLA. A.D. 212

Photogravure Dujardin, Paris

CONSTRUCTION OF WALLS.

PLATE XIII.

FOURTH CENTURY, OR DECADENCE. The construction of this period is very bad, when compared with that of the first three centuries. It is a mixture of stone and brick in alternate layers, and clumsily built. The arches continue to be well turned in brick, nearly the same as in the third century, but with more mortar between them. The example is taken from some of the additions of this period (c. A.D. 300) to the Villa of the Quintilii, on the Via Appia; it is a very good specimen of that kind of construction.

The second example, from the Circus of Maxentius, A.D. 310, is almost equally good, and has the advantage of a positive date from an inscription. This Circus is the only one that remains at all perfect near Rome. It is sometimes called the Circus of Romulus, as Maxentius named it after his son of that name. Other names were formerly given to it before the inscription was found, but there is no longer any doubt about it.

CONSTRUCTION. CENT IV

VILLA QUINTILII, VIA APPIA

CIRCUS OF MAXENTIUS A.D. 310

CONSTRUCTION OF WALLS.

PLATE XIV.

MEDIEVAL BRICKWORK.

1. HOUSE OF S. GREGORY, A.D. 590 (?). The first example is probably rather earlier than the time of S. Gregory, who gave his family mansion to the Church, but it does not follow that he had built it. The construction is very similar to that of the fourth century, but rather inferior to it; A.D. 520 would be a probable date for it, though A.D. 590 is the one usually assigned to the remains of the house given to the Church at that time.

2. CHURCH OF S. STEFANO ROTONDO ON THE CŒLIAN, A.D. 461—483. The brickwork of the original part of this church is better than might have been expected in Rome at that time, and it is probably the work of an architect or builder from Ravenna. The capital shewn in the photograph is quite of the Ravenna type, and of Byzantine character. The arches are well built, though with a good deal of mortar; the filling-up under the arches belongs to a later period.

LATERITIUM, MEDII AEVI

HOUSE OF S GREGORY, A.D. 590

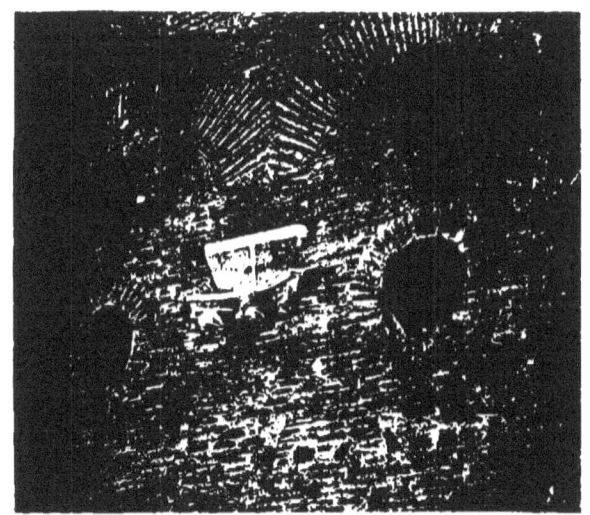

CHURCH OF S STEFANO ROTONDO

PLATE XV.

MEDIEVAL BRICKWORK.

CHURCH OF S. HADRIAN, OR ADRIANO, A.D. 626, in the Forum Romanum. The brickwork of this wall, with the arches of construction in it, belongs to the period of the decay of the Roman art of building, but when there was an attempt to revive it, and it is not a bad imitation of the work of the third century; some parts of the walls of Rome are also of the seventh century, and of similar construction.

THE CHURCH OF S. JOHN AT PORTA LATINA, A.D. 1120; in the hexagonal apse added at that time. This shews another kind of imitation of the old brickwork of the time of the early Empire, after the great revival called Christian art had begun. The sort of plain cornice or corbel-table, shewn in this photograph, is usual in work of the twelfth century in Rome. If this is compared with the corbel-table of a Norman church in England or Normandy, the inferiority of the medieval architecture of Rome to that of England and France at the same period is very evident.

CHURCH OF S JOHN, AT PORTA LATINA. A. D. 1120

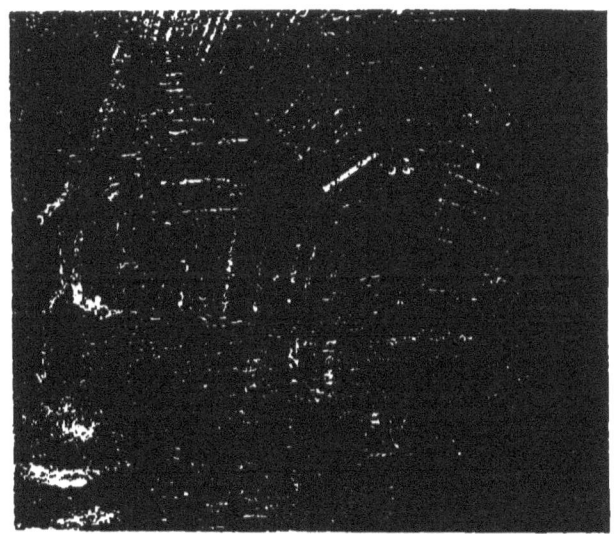

CHURCH OF S HADRIAN IN FORUM A. D. 626

CONSTRUCTION OF WALLS.

PLATE XVI.
OPERA SARACENESCA.

1. MONASTERY OF S. SISTO VECCHIO, *c.* A.D. 1200. 2. CAMPANILE OF S. ROCCO AT FRASCATI, A.D. 1305. This kind of construction is very common in Rome and Italy during the whole medieval period. It is called by this name by the Italian antiquaries, because, according to their traditions, it was brought back to Italy by the Saracens in the construction of their fortresses, chiefly near the sea-shore. If this is true, it is a curious piece of architectural history, as the same construction is found in part of the Villa of Hadrian, at Tivoli (not intended to be seen, but of the time of that Emperor). It is therefore clear that it was used by the Romans in the time of the early Empire, and being a cheap and convenient facing for a rubble wall, was carried by them to Byzantium, and taught to the Saracens in their wars with the later Eastern Empire, and then brought back by them to Italy some centuries afterwards. The example from Frascati is dated by an inscription upon it, which is legible in the photograph.

MONASTERY OF S. SISTO VECCHIO. A.D. 1200

CAMPANILE OF S. ROCCO. FRASCATI A.D. 1305

CONSTRUCTION OF WALLS.

PLATE XVII.

OPUS LATERITIUM, BRICKWORK. It has been pointed out in the text that the best period of brickwork is the time of Nero, where we can measure nine or ten bricks to the foot, and the best examples of this are in the arches of his aqueduct on the Cœlian, which being intended to be seen were carefully worked. A portion of one of these is here given in detail, with the rule to measure them by.

It has been observed that the brickwork of an earlier period is not quite so good, the bricks are thoroughly well made, hard and solid, but not quite so thin as those of his time. It will be seen by those of the PANTHEUM OF AGRIPPA, B.C. 20, given in the upper part of this plate, that there is a decided difference of character, and that the bricks are not so thin.

CONSTRUCTION — OPUS LATERITIUM — BRICK-WORK.

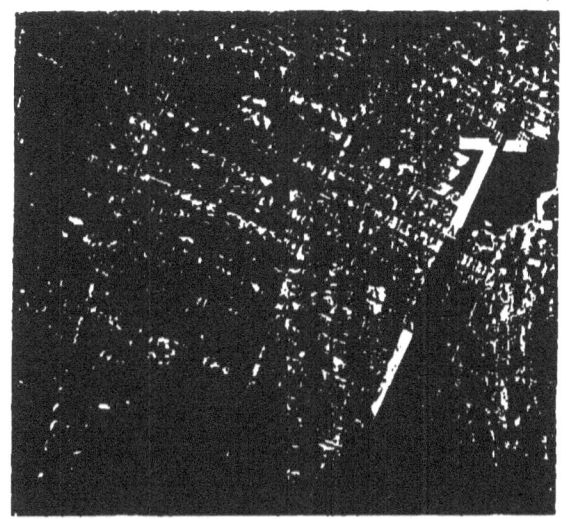

PANTHEUM OF AGRIPPA B.C. 45

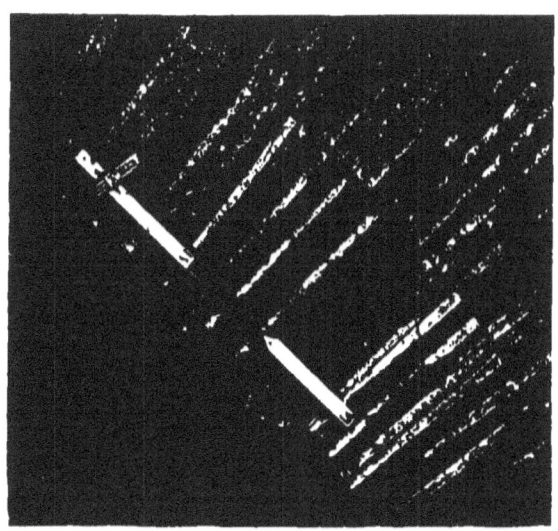

ARCHES OF NERO. A.D. 50

Plate XVIII.

POLYGONAL MASONRY, called also Cyclopean, Pelasgian and Phœnician, Wall of the
    Arcropolis, Mycene, Greece;
    Doorway of Ferentinum, Italy.
    Acropolis of Allatrium, Italy.
    Doorway of Saondos, Asia Minor.

This kind of construction is not found in Rome, because the materials necessary for it are not found there, but an account of the different modes of construction would not be complete without it. This is one of the natural modes of construction, with that kind of stone which will only split into polygonal blocks, and can hardly be cut square. It is found in various parts of the world in volcanic districts, and this sort of natural construction may be of any period. The examples before us are all unquestionably very ancient, in one instance we see Roman masonry built upon earlier Polygonal masonry, yet it is probable that in the same districts the same construction is continued to the present time, because it is the cheapest construction where that material is found. The antiquaries of the last generation did not see this, and bestowed much labour in tracing out this so-called very ancient construction (Pelasgian or Phœnician masonry), and they undoubtedly found many examples of it of early date.

CONSTRUCTION—POLYGONAL MASONRY CALLED ALSO—CYCLOPEAN—PHAENICIAN—OR PELASGIC.

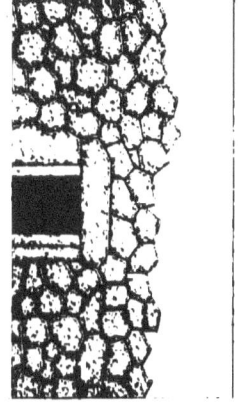

ACROPOLIS OF ALATRIUM—ITALY.

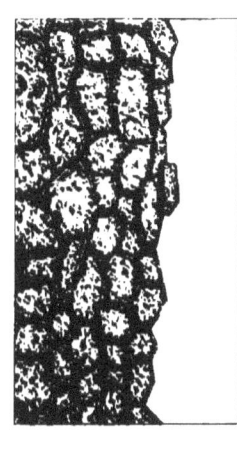

WALL OF ACROPOLIS, MYCENE—GREECE.

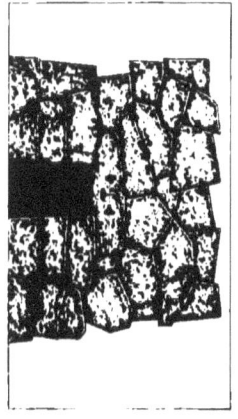

DOORWAY OF SAONDOS—ASIA MINOR.

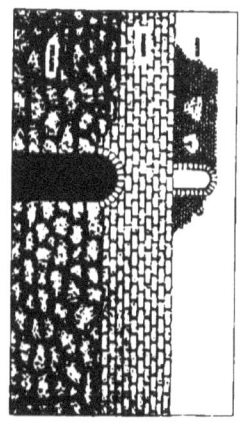

DOORWAY OF FERENTINUM—ITALY.

APPENDIX TO THE CHAPTER

ON THE

HISTORICAL CONSTRUCTION OF WALLS.

MAMERTINE PRISON, &c.

Appendix to the Historical Construction of Walls.

Mamertine Prison.

Plate XIX.

ELEVATION OF PART OF THE UPPER PRISON (on the line G—H on the Plan), as rebuilt in the time of Tiberius, the east front originally facing the Forum of Julius Cæsar, now in the Vicolo del Ghettarello. It has been rebuilt of the old materials, and the lower part of the walls being considered as foundations only (now in the cellars) has not been rebuilt. Modern houses have been built over these cellars, but portions of the wall remain, as shewn in this diagram. The springing-stones, or imposts, on which the arches rest, are of travertine. The arches themselves are of tufa, with the holes left by the iron clamps, indicating the time of Servius Tullius.

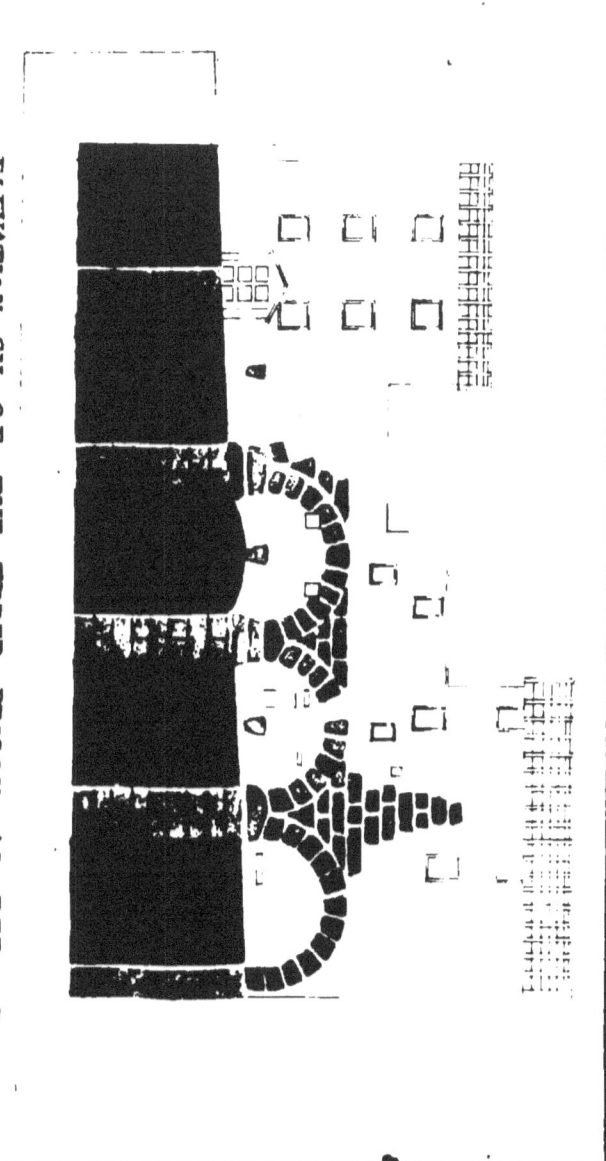

MAMERTINE PRISON

ELEVATION GH. OF THE UPPER PRISON AS REBUILT

APPENDIX TO THE HISTORICAL CONSTRUCTION OF WALLS.

MAMERTINE PRISON.

PLATE XX.

SECTION OF THE CHAMBERS (on the line E—F on the Plan), now cellars. The whole of the construction is of the time of the Kings, but of two periods. The greater part, indeed nearly all, is of the time of Ancus Martius, but one wall is of the time of Servius Tullius, with a straight vertical joint between them. This wall was part of the Robur Tullianum, or strong place of Tullius, the worst part of the prison, the condemned cells. This part was pulled down in the time of Tiberius, and the stones used again. The modern houses built upon these old foundations are shewn in outline only.

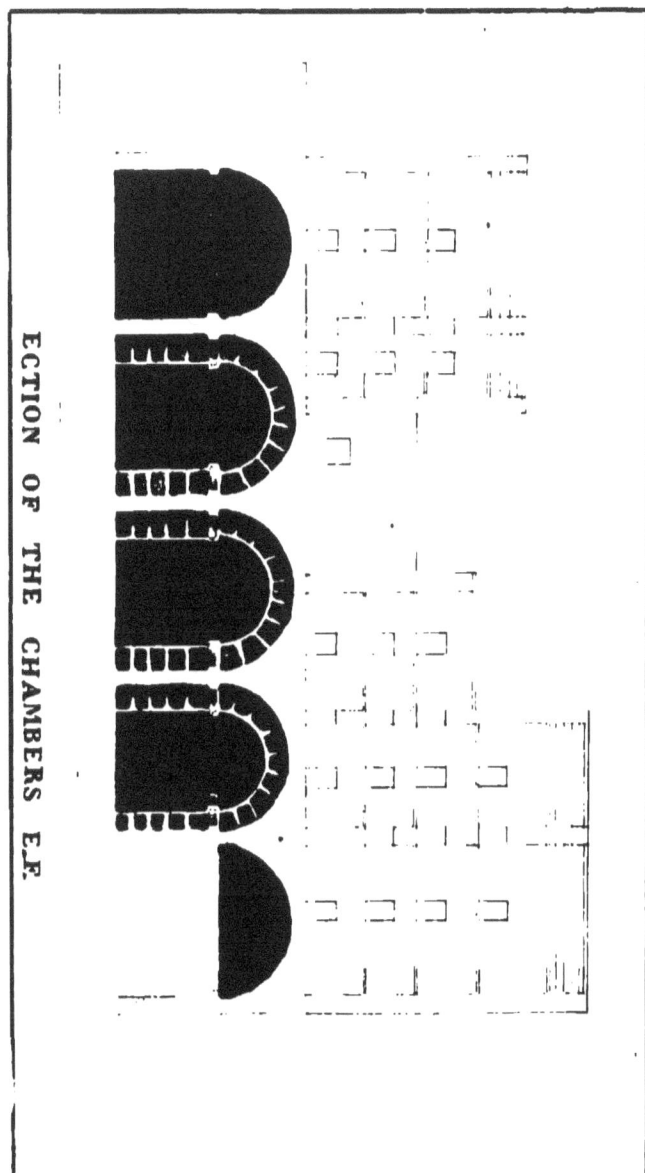

MAMERTINE PRISON

SECTION OF THE CHAMBERS E.F.

APPENDIX TO THE HISTORICAL CONSTRUCTION OF WALLS.

MAMERTINE PRISON.

PLATE XXI.

SECTIONS OF TWO CHAMBERS OF THE PRISON (one marked I—K on the Plan). In this room the depth of the earth with which the floor had been raised is shewn on the left, and a doorway is seen on the original level. The doorway opens into another chamber, still filled with earth, which probably extends to the early passage that passes behind it, but it was dangerous to excavate it any further, as doing so might have let down the modern houses above on the heads of the workmen.

The other Chamber (marked L—M on the Plan). In this an arch is seen which appears to be original, it is filled up with earth nearly to the imposts; the jambs are entirely buried, the depth of the earth is indicated by a faint line. At the back of this arch is a sort of apse, that is to say, the wall is not flat, but slopes out from right to left, where it forms an angle, and this corresponds with a similar angle in the adjoining chamber: the wall between the two runs on to the end of this angle. This singular arrangement is supposed to have been made for some purpose of torture. Near to this arch is a small opening through the wall from the adjoining chamber, apparently to pass provisions through, as there are no stairs to descend into this chamber. There is an opening in the vault by which a person might be let down, and possibly provisions also, though it would be more convenient to pass them through the opening which is close to the arch, and level with a man's arms when standing on the original floor.

MAMERTINE PRISON

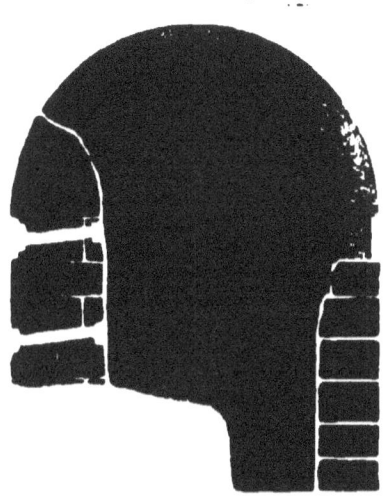

SECTION OF CHAMBER I.K.

SECTION OF CHAMBER L.M.

Appendix to the Historical Construction of Walls.

Mamertine Prison.

Plate XXII.

SECTION OF THE PASSAGE (marked C—D on the Plan). This passage is of the early Etruscan character, such as might be expected in the time of King Ancus Martius. The walls over the vault are built of the large stones usual at the period, and the vault is semi-octagon, not semi-circular.

SECTION OF THE CLOACA MAXIMA. The construction of this is exactly the same as that of the passage, and both were built by the same king, according to Livy. The Cloaca appears less lofty than the passage, because the lower part of it is concealed by the water; the bottom of it is also raised considerably by filling up with a deposit of mud. There is a connection between the two, as the passage is over a drain that leads into the great Cloaca, and one use of it probably was to enable the watermen to keep the drain clear.

MAMERTINE PRISON

SECTION OF THE PASSAGE C.D.

SECTION OF THE CLOACA MAXIMA

APPENDIX TO CONSTRUCTION OF WALLS.

CAPITOLIUM, &c.

Construction of Walls.

Plate I.
1. Part of the Wall at the West End.

This end is the oldest part, the east end has been rebuilt after the great fire in the time of Sylla. The construction of the Ærarium is the same as this earliest part, but on the exterior a portion of it has been faced with smaller square stones, probably in the time of King Theodoric, who repaired many of the public buildings in Rome. The original part is now the same as it was in the time of Terentius Varro, who wrote nearly a century before the Christian era. He says that it was considered in his time to have belonged to the City of the Sabines, on the hill of Saturn, before the arrival of the Romans, but the construction is *fine-jointed*, as is shewn in the photograph, and therefore of later date than the rude *wide-jointed* masonry of Roma Quadrata on the Palatine. All the original parts of this great public building are of the same construction. There is every probability that it was erected by the Romans and the Sabines jointly, to contain the public offices of the new City, when it was enclosed in one wall. The stones are cut with the saw, those on the Palatine are not.

CAPITOLIUM, TABULARIUM, MUNICIPIUM, ETC. CONSTRUCTION

CONSTRUCTION OF WALLS.

PLATE II.

THIS plate represents the details of one of the arches at the back of the TABULARIUM, an addition to the original fabric, as is shewn by the straight vertical joints at the junction of the two walls. This arcade, by the name of *porticus*, is frequently mentioned by the Classical writers. The stone has been considerably eaten away in parts, at the time when that great building was a salt warehouse in the Middle Ages, but in other parts the salt has not reached the stone, and it remains in a genuine state and entirely unaltered. It is therefore a good example of the construction of the second period of the Kings of Rome.

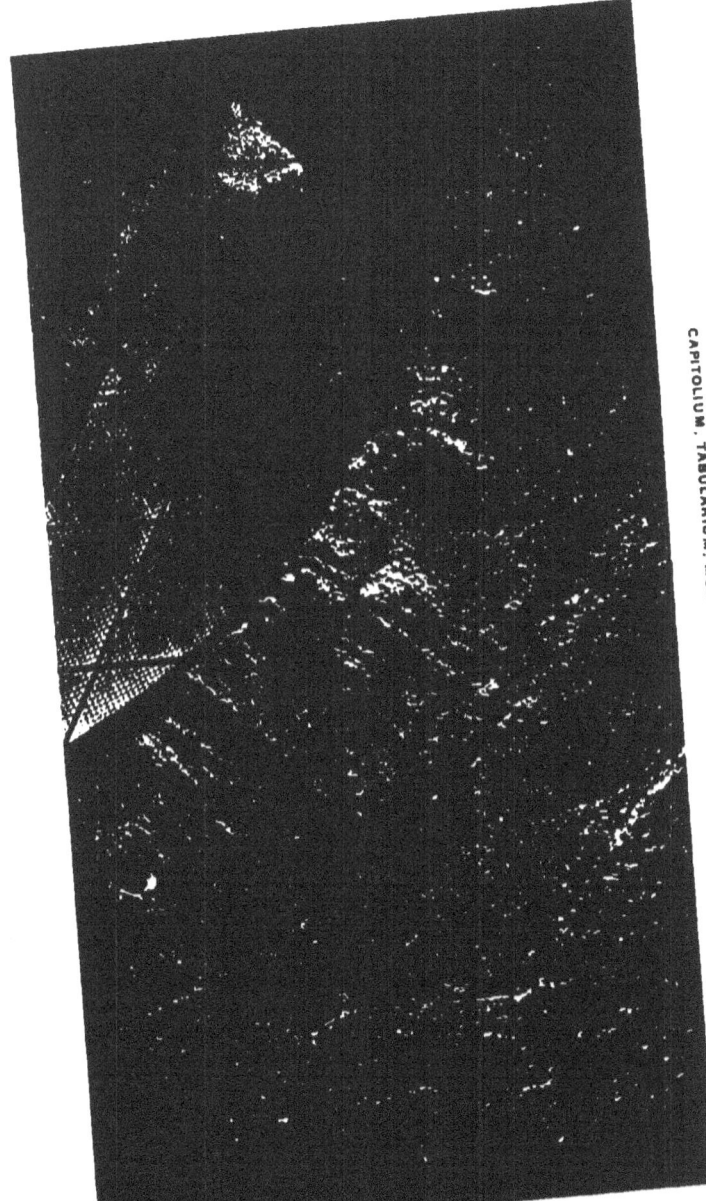

CAPITOLIUM, TABULARIUM, MUNICIPIUM, ETC. CONSTRUCTION

PLATE III.

THIS plate represents the east end as rebuilt by Sylla, and mentioned by Pliny as the substructure of the Capitolium. It appears to have been rebuilt of the old square stones, at least they are of the same large size and have the same fine joints.

In making the new steps and sloping path from the Arch of Septimius Severus the lower part of this great wall has been undermined, as is clearly seen in this view. The original steps from the great prison to the Senaculum, or the Law Courts, were to the north or left end of this view, probably on the same site as the steps that now go down on the north side of the "Prison of S. Peter." Beyond this, in this photograph, the Arch of Septimius Severus is indistinctly seen on the lower ground.

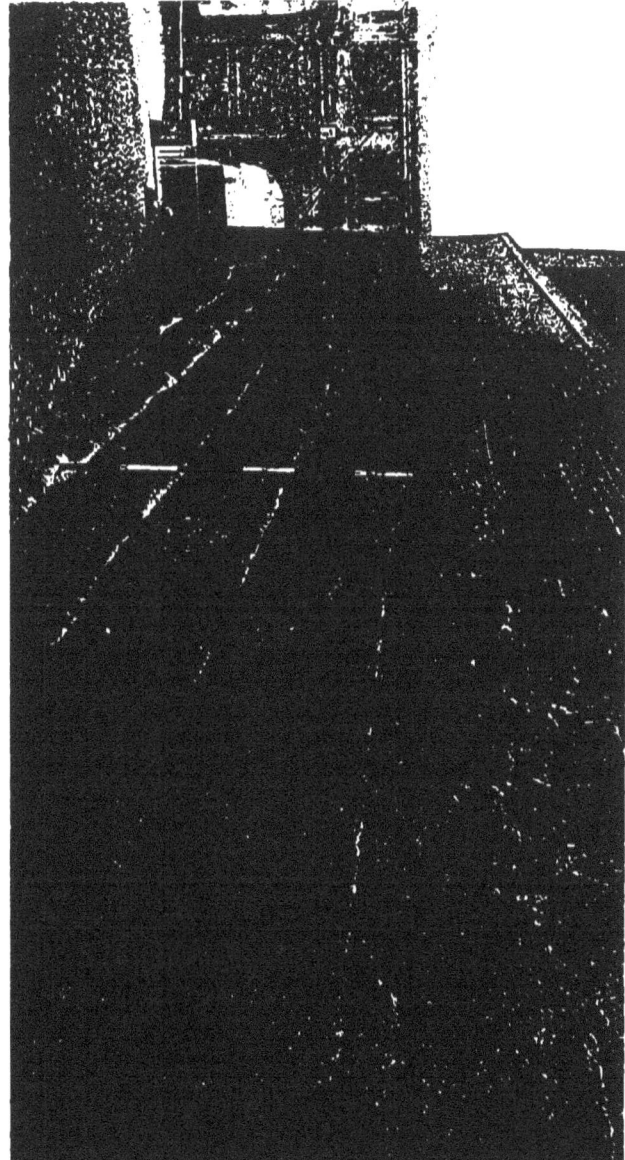

CAPITOLIUM, TABULARIUM, MUNICIPIUM, ETC. CONSTRUCTION

PLATE IV.

This plate represents the one arch of the Porticus of the Tabularium that is now left open, with the rude Tuscan pilasters or half pillars. These arches were walled-up by Michael Angelo at the time that he rebuilt in stone the upper stories, which had previously been of wood. Under this, one of the windows of the Ærarium is shewn, and a part of the wall faced with small square stones, as has been mentioned, probably of the time of King Theodoric. All this part of the building was either buried in earth or concealed by medieval buildings erected against it, at the time when Michael Angelo rebuilt the upper part. He considered the substructure as foundations only, and it is in that manner that they have escaped rebuilding.

TABULARIUM. AERARIUM

DESCRIPTION OF THE DIAGRAMS

OF THE

CAPITOLIUM,

CONTAINING THE

ÆRARIUM, TABULARIUM, SENACULUM,
AND MUNICIPIUM.

CAPITOLIUM, MUNICIPIUM, &c.

PLATE I.

THE NORTH FRONT, BY MICHAEL ANGELO. This front faces the open space on the Capitoline Hill, now called *Piazza del Campidoglio*, originally called the AREA CAPITOLINA. On this side the building is only two storeys high. On the southern side (shewn below) it is five storeys high: this front faces the Forum Romanum. In this elevation the old walls are represented in a dark tint, the modern walls in a light one, and this plan is followed in the whole of the eight plates of this remarkable building. Before the time of Michael Angelo the two upper floors, occupied by the Municipality, had always been of wood only, and in order to support the weight of the stone walls he thought it necessary to fill up the arches of the Tabularium, one of which only has since been opened. The tower at the south-east corner of the building, shewn on the right of the view, is medieval. Michael Angelo found it there, and did not disturb it. Like all the other ancient buildings of Rome, this was turned into a castle in the Middle Ages. The lower part of this had been buried for centuries, and houses built up against the walls of this great ancient public building, for which reason the architect did not consider the appearance on this side, not expecting it to be seen.

The ground-plan at the foot of this plate shews that it is mainly rock, with passages partly cut in it, and partly built up against it. The Ærarium, shewn in front, was divided into small square chambers by wooden partitions, with one small window in each; this was equivalent to the bank-vaults for coin in the Bank of England. It is said by Numismatists that the coins of Servius Tullius were made square, in order to pack better into these square vaults, and that some of these were found there by Julius Cæsar when he robbed the Public Treasury. The coins of Servius Tullius are common in all collections of coins, and are the earliest Roman coins. The straight passage cut into the rock, to the left of the plan, is the staircase of the ÆRARIUM, for the use of the treasury clerks, mentioned by Cicero[a], the ascent of which is compared by him to "climbing the Alps," and the steps are as steep as they well could be. On the right-hand side is another staircase, but winding, and of easy ascent, leading up to the SENACULUM or Senate-house; the passage leading to these steps passes under the platform of the Temple of Concord: that of the ÆRARIUM or Treasury passes under the platform of the Temple of Saturn.

[a] Oratio pro Fonteio, c. i. 4.

CAPITOLIUM, MUNICIPIUM, &c.

NORTH FRONT. BY MICHAEL ANGELO.

SOUTH FRONT, ÆRARIUM, TABULARIUM, AND MUNICIPIUM.

PLAN OF THE GROUND-FLOOR, WITH THE ÆRARIUM AND THE TWO STAIRCASES.

Plate II.

PLANS OF THE SECOND AND THIRD FLOORS. On the second floor the Tabularium is seen in front, with various chambers behind it, the walls of which are of the original construction; they are now cellars or warehouses only. To the left is the present entrance, with the modern staircase up to the offices of the Municipality; a part of the staircase of the Ærarium, for the treasury clerks, is also seen within this, and further back another modern staircase is seen to the left, for the upper rooms. On the right is the wall of substructure mentioned with praise by Pliny, a part of which has been preserved from having been long underground; the upper part has been carried away for building-materials, and in front of it the earth has been dug away to make the modern sloping path and steps down to the Arch of Septimius Severus, so that the wall is almost undermined.

The line of the Section of the southern portion, which forms Plate VIII., is marked A—B on the plan.

On the third floor, under the other on the plate, the GREAT HALL OF THE MUNICIPALITY, marked N—N, is shewn, with small chambers behind it, marked G G G; a small internal staircase to an upper storey is marked H; an internal passage and offices, I I I; the lofty central tower, E; small central courtyards, P P; other staircase to the upper floor, O.O O; and rooms for the astronomer in the tower, B B B.

CAPITOLIUM, MUNICIPIUM, &c. 2.

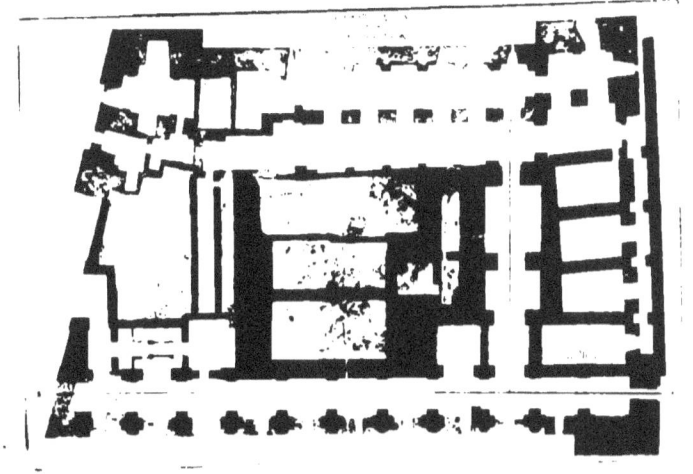

PLAN OF SECOND FLOOR, WITH THE TABULARIUM, &c.

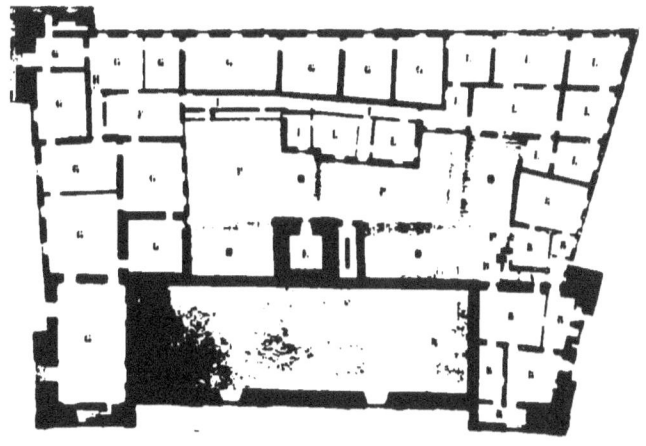

PLAN OF THIRD FLOOR, WITH THE SENACULUM, &c.

CAPITOLIUM, MUNICIPIUM, &c.

PLATE III.

ELEVATION ON THE WEST SIDE, WITH THE SUBSTRUCTURE. It will be seen that the greater part of the building on this side is modern; the ancient part consists only of that which is dark on the plate, but the construction of this part is some of the earliest in the whole building. The central opening is the present entrance to the Municipal offices, and is in daily use. The construction of the walls belongs to the second period of the Walls of the Kings, and is part of the work mentioned by Terentius Varro as being undertaken in his time (B.C. 50), and had been part of one of the buildings that had belonged to the city of the Sabines before the arrival of the Romans [a]. It is far more probable that it was erected immediately after the union of the Romans with the Sabines, for the public offices of the new city, the future greatness of which was foretold by the leaders and kings from the beginning. For details of the construction, see Plates I. and II. of the Photo-engravings of the Capitolium, &c., in the Appendix to the chapter on the Historical Construction of Walls.

ELEVATION OF THE EAST SIDE, WITH THE SUBSTRUCTURE. The substructure on this side is of much later character than that on the western side, and is of the time of Sylla, mentioned by Pliny with great praise. The manner in which the ground has been cut away is very clearly seen in this view. The medieval tower at the angle is near to the Arch of Septimius Severus, and the Temple of Concord is just under it, on the southern side. For details of the construction of the substructure, see Plate III. of the Photo-engravings of this building.

[a] Ter. Varro, de Ling. Lat., l. v. c. 7.

CAPITOLIUM, MUNICIPIUM, &c. 3.

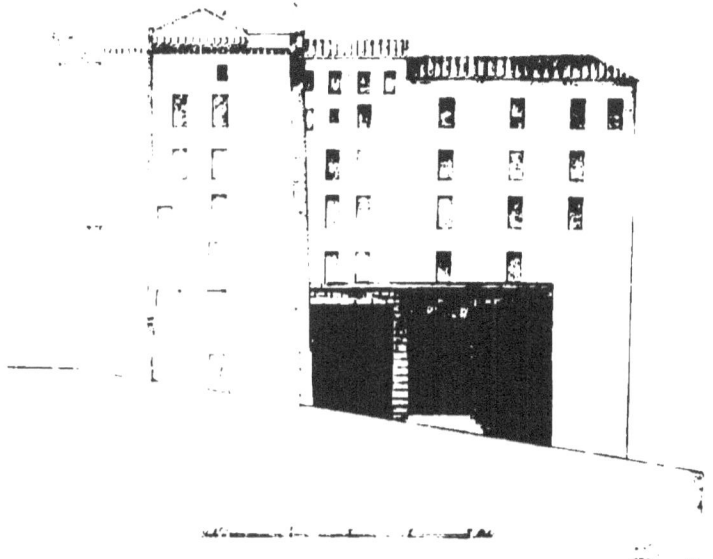

ELEVATION OF WEST SIDE, WITH THE SUBSTRUCTURE.

ELEVATION OF EAST SIDE, WITH THE SUBSTRUCTURE.

Capitolium, Municipium, &c.

Plate IV.

Section of East Side, with the Stairs of the Senaculum.

The platform of the Temple of Concord is also shewn in front of this, with the passage under it leading to these stairs. The section of the Ærarium is thus seen where the steps are, over that the section of the Tabularium. Behind this are original vaulted chambers, and over them the hall of the Senaculum, or Senate-house, to which this staircase leads; the upper part of this has been destroyed. To the right are seen the steps of Michael Angelo, in front of his building, leading up to the state apartments of the Municipality, with the statues; the third, or intermediate floor, is between the two storeys, one of ancient stone buildings below, the other of modern buildings above; this intermediate storey was much damaged by the great fire in the time of Sylla, but a great part of the walls are ancient.

Section of the West Side, with the Stairs of the Ærarium, and the Temple of Saturn at the foot.

Under the platform of this temple is the passage to the steps of the Ærarium; and, as we are told that in the time of Sylla the Ærarium was turned into the Temple of Saturn[a], it is evident that they were closely connected. Modern topographers usually call this temple that of Vespasian, but the one in front of it, which is more perfect, answers to that; the present structures are probably both of his time. The section of the Ærarium or Tabularium is again seen behind the temple, as also the steep steps, with the vaults over them; and the offices of the Municipality above.

[a] Solinus, c. 2; Servius in Virgilii Georgica, v. 502.

CAPITOLIUM, MUNICIPIUM, &c.

Section of East Side, with the Stairs of the Senaculum.

Section of West Side, with the Stairs of the Ærarium, and the Temple of Saturn at the Foot.

CAPITOLIUM, MUNICIPIUM, &c.

PLATE V.

SECTION OF THE PORTICUS AT THE WEST END, with the Modern Stairs.

These modern stairs are the present approach to the Municipal offices. The porticus or arcade was continued along the eastern side of the great building, and is of very early construction, but not quite so early as the Ærarium and Tabularium on the southern side. It was built up against them very soon afterwards, and still belongs to the second period of the Walls of the Kings. This porticus is mentioned several times by Classical authors, especially in the time of the great fire recorded by Tacitus[a].

SECTION AT THE EAST END, SHEWING THE SENACULUM, with Modern Changes.

This floor had been much damaged in the great fire in the time of Sylla, as has been mentioned; only part of this wall is old, as it was entirely disregarded by Michael Angelo, and thus it is very difficult to make it out with any certainty. Over this are remains of a great hall, to which the steps from the passage under the Temple of Concord had led up, (although the upper part has been cut off). The building has been much altered at this end, and the present wall does not rest on the old substructure, but a passage is left behind it. It was at one period allowed to be inhabited by poor cottagers; and the steps marked in the wall in the centre of this drawing lead up to an upper chamber, made under the vault of the old hall.

[a] Hist. i. 2, and iii. 72.

CAPITOLIUM, MUNICIPIUM, &c. 5.

SECTION OF PORTICUS AT THE WEST END, WITH MODERN STAIRS.

SECTION AT EAST END, SHEWING THE SENACULUM, WITH MODERN CHANGES.

CAPITOLIUM, MUNICIPIUM, &c.

PLATE VI.

SECTION THROUGH THE CENTRE, WITH THE ANCIENT SUBSTRUCTURE AND THE MODERN TOWER. In this section the different levels of the ground come out very clearly, with the platform of the Temple of Concord at the foot to the left on the low level, the steps of Michael Angelo to the right on the high level, and the distinction between the old walls and the modern ones marked by the different tints. The celebrated tower of the Capitol in the centre is modern, or at least of the time of Michael Angelo; it commands the finest view of Rome, being exactly in the centre of the City, and the highest point in it.

INTERNAL ELEVATION OF THE TABULARIUM AND ÆRARIUM, WITH THE DOORS TO THE STAIRS. In this elevation the ancient work only is shewn; the substructure is also shewn in detail in Plate IV. of the Photo-engravings of this building. The doorways, as will be seen, are cut through the rock under the Ærarium; and the passages from these to the foot of the slope pass under the Ærarium, having previously passed under the platforms of the Temple of Concord, or of Saturn, before they arrived at these doorways.

CAPITOLIUM, MUNICIPIUM, &c. 6.

SECTION THROUGH THE CENTRE, WITH THE ANCIENT SUBSTRUCTURE AND THE MODERN TOWER.

ELEVATION OF TABULARIUM AND ÆRARIUM, WITH DOORS TO STAIRS.

CAPITOLIUM, MUNICIPIUM, &c.

PLATE VII.

PLAN ON THE LEVEL OF THE TABULARIUM. Part of the object of this plan is to shew the exact situation with reference to the Forum Romanum, by so well-known an object as the Arch of Septimius Severus, marked D in the plan. This stands in the Forum, and near one of the triumphal arches on the Via Sacra, at the foot of the ascent to the Capitoline Hill. The Temple of Concord is shewn immediately behind this; that temple was not in the Forum, but in the Capitol: the boundary between the two was the paved road, made, as usual, in the foss of the old fortifications of the Hill of Saturn. The temple immediately on the left of the Arch is that of Vespasian (usually miscalled of Saturn); the one behind it is that of Saturn, and in the corner, at the angle with a bend, is that of the Dei Consenti, or household gods of Rome: at the junction of the two roads, between the temples of Concord and Saturn, was the gate of the fortress of the hill of Saturn; this, with the Temple of Saturn, as it then stood, and the Tabularium, form the three buildings which Terentius Varro states were in his time considered to have belonged to the city of the Sabines, which shew that they were of very early and rude construction. The Temple of Saturn was rebuilt by Vespasian. Behind this are the great buildings at that level, with a central court and buildings all round it; the steps on the right-hand side are modern. The wall up to the Capitol on the left is also modern, (and is about to be destroyed). The old paved road passed under it, and went on as far as the Temple of Jupiter Capitolinus, (now in the garden of the German Embassy); and then turning at a right angle to the Arca Capitolina. This plan is taken from Canina.

CAPITOLIUM, MUNICIPIUM, &c.   7.
PLAN ON THE LEVEL OF THE TABULARIUM.

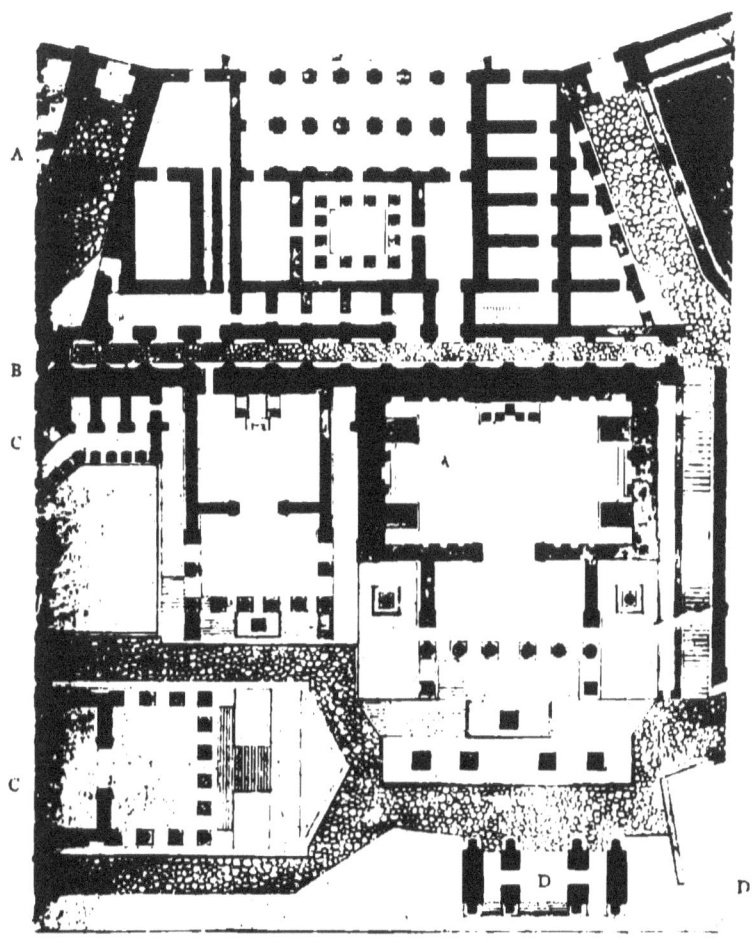

A. Municipium.   B. Tabularium.   C. Temples.
D. Arch of Septimius Severus.

CAPITOLIUM, MUNICIPIUM, &c.

PLATE VIII.

SECTION OF SOUTH FRONT, LOOKING SOUTH. The line of this Section is marked upon the Plan which forms Plate II. by the line A—B. The elevation of this part separately has already been given in Plate VI., but this gives the best general idea of the whole building; one is of great historical importance from its great antiquity, which is borne out by the substructure shewn in Plate IV. of the Photo-engravings of this building. At the foot of the Section, those of the three temples against the wall of the Ærarium are also given. These are above the level of the Forum Romanum, and were originally separated from it by a wall or a foss, as we have seen. The remains of the Comitium, recently found, are at a considerably lower level, below the base of the Arch of Septimius Severus; and there must have been steps down to it (though they have not yet been found, probably because they are under the modern road). This building is nearly due north of the Forum Romanum, but *not quite*, and this makes it doubtful whether the public offices within it were called the Curia or not, as Pliny expressly says[a] that the Curia was *due north* of the Forum. Immediately to the east of this great pile of buildings are the remains of the prison of the Kings, popularly called the Mamertine Prison, and this must be *due north* of the Forum. As the chambers of the prison hitherto found have been entirely subterranean, it seems not improbable that the Law Courts, properly called the CURIA, were built over the prison, in the same manner as the Municipal Offices are over the Tabularium. There is reason to believe that the prison formed three sides of a quadrangle, of which the fourth side was open to the Forum; this would agree both with Pliny and with Vitruvius.

[a] Plinii Nat. Hist., vii. 66.

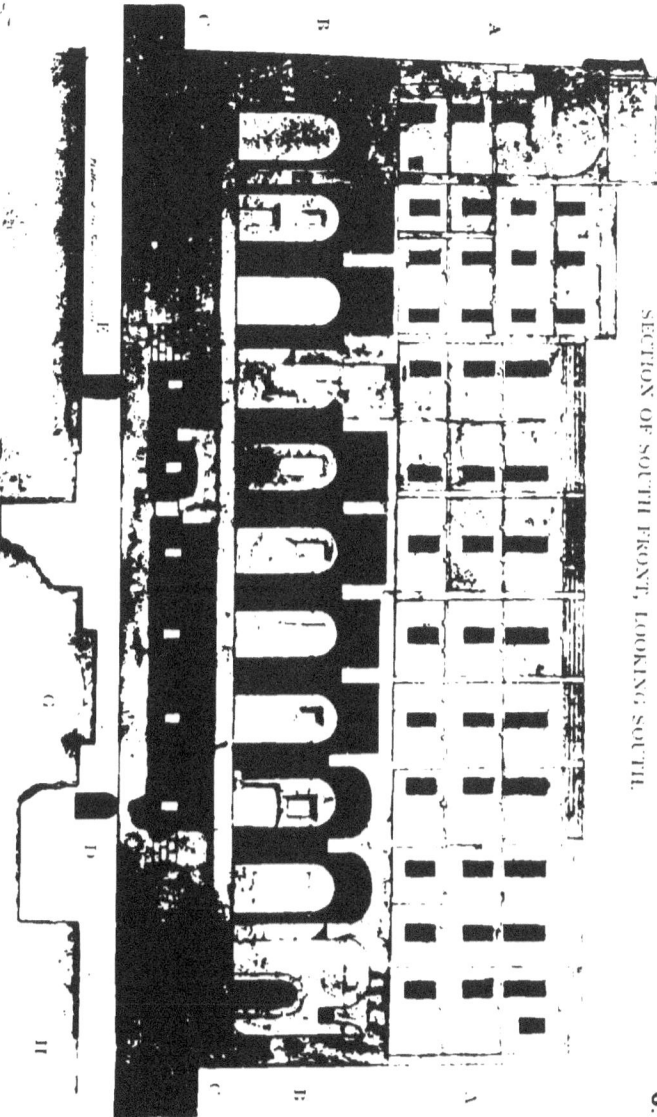

CAPITOLIUM. ÆRARIUM. TABULARIUM. MUNICIPIUM.
SECTION OF SOUTH FRONT, LOOKING SOUTH.

A. Municipium. B. Tabularium. C. Ærarium. D. Door of Ærarium. E. Door of Senaculum. F G H. Temples.

8.

WORKS ON
Mediæval Architecture and Archæology,

PUBLISHED BY

JAMES PARKER AND CO.
OXFORD, AND 377, STRAND, LONDON.

THE GLOSSARY OF ARCHITECTURE ABRIDGED.

A CONCISE GLOSSARY OF TERMS USED IN GRECIAN, ROMAN, ITALIAN, AND GOTHIC ARCHITECTURE. By JOHN HENRY PARKER, C.B., M.A., F.S.A. A New Edition, revised. Fcap. 8vo., with 470 Illustrations, in ornamental cloth, price 7s. 6d.

ARCHITECTURAL MANUAL.

AN INTRODUCTION TO THE STUDY OF GOTHIC ARCHITECTURE.

By JOHN HENRY PARKER, C.B., M.A., F.S.A. *Fourth Edition*, Revised and Enlarged, with 180 Illustrations, and a Glossarial Index. Fcap. 8vo., in ornamental cloth, price 5s.

ARCHÆOLOGICAL HANDBOOK.

THE ARCHÆOLOGIST'S HANDBOOK. By HENRY GODWIN, F.S.A.—This work contains a summary of the materials which are available for the investigation of the Monuments of this country, arranged chiefly under their several successive periods, from the earliest times to the fifteenth century,—together with Tables of Dates, Kings, &c., Lists of Coins, Cathedrals, Castles, Monasteries, &c. Crown 8vo., cloth, price 7s. 6d.

THE ARCHÆOLOGY OF ROME.

THE ARCHÆOLOGY OF ROME. By JOHN HENRY PARKER, C.B., M.A., F.S.A. Medium 8vo. Illustrated by Plans, Wood Engravings, &c. [*Vol. II. nearly ready.*

MEDIÆVAL GLASS PAINTING.

AN INQUIRY INTO THE DIFFERENCE OF STYLE OBSERVABLE IN ANCIENT GLASS PAINTINGS, especially in England, with Hints on Glass Painting, by the late CHARLES WINSTON. With Corrections and Additions by the Author. *A New Edition.* 2 vols., Medium 8vo., with numerous coloured Engravings, cloth, £1 11s. 6d.

CHRIST'S HOSPITAL, ABINGDON.

A MONUMENT OF CHRISTIAN MUNIFICENCE; or, An Account of the Brotherhood of the Holy Cross, and of the Hospital of Christ in Abingdon, by FRANCIS LITTLE, 1627. Edited, with a Preface and Appendix, from the MS. in the possession of the Governors of the Hospital, by CLAUDE DELAVAL COBHAM, B.C.L., M.A. Fcap. 8vo., toned paper, cloth, 4s.

MEDIÆVAL BRASSES.

A MANUAL OF MONUMENTAL BRASSES. Comprising an Introduction to the Study of these Memorials, and a List of those remaining in the British Isles. With Two Hundred Illustrations. By the late Rev. HERBERT HAINES, M.A., of Exeter College, Oxford. 2 vols., 8vo., price 21s.

MEDIÆVAL ARMOUR.

ANCIENT ARMOUR AND WEAPONS IN EUROPE. By JOHN HEWITT, Member of the Archæological Institute of Great Britain. The work complete, from the Iron Period of the Northern Nations to the Seventeenth Century. 3 vols., 8vo., 2l. 10s.

EARLY BRITISH ARCHÆOLOGY.

OUR BRITISH ANCESTORS: WHO AND WHAT WERE THEY? An Inquiry serving to elucidate the Traditional History of the Early Britons by means of recent Excavations, Etymology, Remnants of Religious Worship, Inscriptions, &c. By the Rev. SAMUEL LYSONS, M.A., F.S.A., Rector of Rodmarton. Post 8vo., cloth, 12s.

MEDIÆVAL SKETCH-BOOK.

FACSIMILE OF THE SKETCH-BOOK OF WILARS DE HONECORT, AN ARCHITECT OF THE THIRTEENTH CENTURY. With Commentaries and Descriptions by MM. LASSUS and QUICHERAT. Translated and Edited by the Rev. ROBERT WILLIS, M.A., F.R.S., Jacksonian Professor at Cambridge, &c. With 64 Facsimiles, 10 Illustrative Plates, and 43 Woodcuts. Royal 4to., cloth, 2l. 10s. *The English letterpress separate, for the purchasers of the French edition,* 4to., 15s.

ARCHITECTURE.

MEDIÆVAL DOMESTIC ARCHITECTURE.

SOME ACCOUNT OF DOMESTIC ARCHITECTURE IN ENGLAND, from Richard II. to Henry VIII. (or the Perpendicular Style). With numerous Illustrations of Existing Remains from Original Drawings. By the EDITOR OF "THE GLOSSARY OF ARCHITECTURE." In 2 vols., 8vo., 1*l*. 10*s*.

Also,

FROM EDWARD I. TO RICHARD II. (the Edwardian Period, or the Decorated Style). 8vo., cloth, 21*s*.

MEDIÆVAL CASTLES.

THE MILITARY ARCHITECTURE OF THE MIDDLE AGES. Translated from the French of M. VIOLLET-LE-DUC, by M. MACDERMOTT, Esq., Architect. With 151 original French Engravings. Medium 8vo., cloth, 21*s*.

GOTHIC ARCHITECTURE.

AN ATTEMPT TO DISCRIMINATE THE STYLES OF ARCHITECTURE IN ENGLAND, FROM THE CONQUEST TO THE REFORMATION: with a Sketch of the Grecian and Roman Orders. By the late THOMAS RICKMAN, F.S.A. *Sixth Edition*, with considerable Additions, chiefly Historical, by JOHN HENRY PARKER, C.B., M.A., F.S.A., and numerous Illustrations. Medium 8vo. [*Reprinting.*

MEDIÆVAL IRONWORK.

SERRURERIE DU MOYEN-AGE, Par RAYMOND BORDEAUX. Forty Lithographic Plates, by G. Bouet, and numerous Woodcuts. Small 4to., cloth, 20*s*.

MEDIÆVAL SCULPTURE.

A SERIES OF MANUALS OF GOTHIC ORNAMENT. No. 1. STONE CARVING; 2. MOULDINGS; 3. SURFACE ORNAMENT. 16mo., price 1*s*. each.

ENGLISH COUNTRY HOUSES.

FORTY-FIVE VIEWS AND PLANS of recently-erected Mansions, Private Residences, Parsonage-Houses, Farm-Houses, Lodges, and Cottages; with the actual cost of each, and A PRACTICAL TREATISE ON HOUSE-BUILDING. By WILLIAM WILKINSON, Architect, Oxford. Royal 4to., ornamental cloth, price £1 16*s*.

ARCHITECTURAL TOPOGRAPHY.

ENGLISH COUNTIES.

OR, AN ARCHITECTURAL ACCOUNT OF EVERY CHURCH IN

BEDFORDSHIRE, 2s. 6d.
BERKSHIRE, 2s. 6d.
BUCKINGHAMSHIRE, 2s. 6d.
CAMBRIDGESHIRE, 4s.
HUNTINGDONSHIRE, 2s. 6d.
OXFORDSHIRE, 2s. 6d.

SUFFOLK, with Engravings, 7s. 6d.

Its Dedication.—Supposed date of Erection or Alteration.—Objects of Interest in or near.—Notices of Fonts.—Glass, Furniture, —and other details.—Also Lists of Dated Examples, Works relating to the County, &c.

N.B. Each Church has been personally surveyed for the occasion by some competent antiquary.

ENGLISH CATHEDRALS.

THE ARCHITECTURAL HISTORY OF CANTERBURY CATHEDRAL. By Professor WILLIS, M.A., F.R.S, &c. With Woodcuts and Plans. 8vo., cloth, 10s. 6d.

THE ARCHITECTURAL HISTORY OF YORK CATHEDRAL. By Professor WILLIS, M.A., F.R.S., &c. With Woodcuts and Plans. 8vo., 2s. 6d.

WESTMINSTER ABBEY.

GLEANINGS FROM WESTMINSTER ABBEY. By GEORGE GILBERT SCOTT, R.A., F.S.A. With Appendices supplying Further Particulars, and completing the History of the Abbey Buildings, by Several Writers. *Second Edition, enlarged, containing many new Illustrations by O. Jewitt and others.* Medium 8vo., cloth, gilt top, price 15s.

WELLS.

THE ARCHITECTURAL ANTIQUITIES OF THE CITY OF WELLS. By JOHN HENRY PARKER, C.B., M.A., F.S.A. Illustrated by Plans and Views. Medium 8vo., cloth, price 5s.

ILLUSTRATIONS OF ARCHITECTURAL ANTIQUITIES.

WELLS: 32 Photographs, Folio size, in portfolio, price 3l. 3s.; or separately, 2s. 6d. each.
Also 16 Photographs, in 8vo., reduced from the above, in a case, price 15s.; or separately, 1s. each.

GLASTONBURY ABBEY: 9 Photographs, Folio size, in portfolio, price 1l.; or separately, 2s. 6d. each.

DORSETSHIRE: 23 Photographs, Folio size, in portfolio, price 4l. 4s.; or separately, 2s. 6d. each.

ENGLISH TOPOGRAPHY.

OXFORD.—A HAND-BOOK FOR VISITORS TO
OXFORD. Illustrated by One Hundred and Twenty-eight Woodcuts by Jewitt, and Twenty-nine Steel Plates by Le Keux. A New Edition. 8vo. [*Reprinting.*

—— **THE RAILWAY TRAVELLER'S WALK**
THROUGH OXFORD. *A New Edition, with Fifty-six Illustrations.* 18mo., in ornamental wrapper, 1s.

—— **GUIDE to ARCHITECTURAL ANTIQUI-**
TIES in the Neighbourhood of Oxford. 8vo., cloth, 12s.

CHESTER.—THE MEDIÆVAL ARCHITECTURE
OF CHESTER. By JOHN HENRY PARKER, C.B., M.A., F.S.A. With an Historical Introduction by the Rev. FRANCIS GROSVENOR. Illustrated by Engravings. 8vo., cloth, 5s.

DOVER.—THE CHURCH AND FORTRESS OF
DOVER CASTLE. By the Rev. JOHN PUCKLE, M.A., Vicar of St. Mary's, Dover. With Illustrations from the Author's Drawings. Medium 8vo., cloth, 7s. 6d.

NORTHAMPTON.—ARCHITECTURAL NOTICES
of the CHURCHES in the ARCHDEACONRY of NORTHAMPTON. With numerous Illustrations on Wood and Steel. Royal 8vo., cloth, 1l. 1s.

DURHAM.—ILLUSTRATIONS OF THE MEDI-
ÆVAL ANTIQUITIES OF THE COUNTY OF DURHAM. By J. TAVENOR PERRY and CHARLES HENMAN, Jun., Architects. (Dedicated by permission to the Duke of Cleveland.) Super-royal Folio, on toned paper, in wrapper, £1 11s. 6d.

WOODSTOCK.—THE EARLY HISTORY of WOOD-
STOCK MANOR and its Environs, in Bladon, Hensington, New Woodstock, Blenheim; With later Notices: By EDWARD MARSHALL, M.A., formerly Fellow of C.C.C., Oxford; Diocesan Inspector of Schools for the Deanery of Woodstock. Post 8vo., cloth, 12s.

By the same Author,

SANDFORD.—AN ACCOUNT of the PARISH OF
SANDFORD, in the Deanery of Woodstock, Oxon. Crown 8vo., cloth, 3s.

CHURCH ENSTONE.—AN ACCOUNT of the TOWN-
SHIP OF CHURCH ENSTONE, in the Deanery of Chipping-Norton, Oxon. Crown 8vo., cloth, 3s.

IFFLEY.—A HISTORY OF THE TOWNSHIP OF
IFFLEY, OXFORDSHIRE. Crown 8vo. A New Edition. [*Nearly ready.*

WORKING DRAWINGS.

WORKING DRAWINGS OF CHURCHES, WITH VIEWS, ELEVATIONS, SECTIONS, AND DETAILS.

WARMINGTON CHURCH. Royal folio, cloth, 10s. 6d.
A fine thirteenth-century Church. About 115 feet by 47.

SAINT LEONARD'S, KIRKSTEAD. Small folio, 5s.
A small Church in the Early English style. 42 feet by 19.

MINSTER LOVELL CHURCH. Folio, 5s.
A very elegant specimen of the Perpendicular style. To hold 350 persons.

LITTLEMORE CHURCH. *Second Edition*, with the designs of the painted Glass Windows. Folio, 5s.
A small modern Church, in the Early English style. Size, 60 feet by 55, and 40 feet high. Cost 600l. Holds 210 persons.

SHOTTESBROKE CHURCH. Folio, 3s. 6d.
A good and pure specimen of the Decorated style.

WILCOTE CHURCH. Folio, 3s. 6d.
A small Church in the Decorated style. Size, 50 feet by 20. Estimated cost, 304l. Holds 160 persons.

ST. BARTHOLOMEW'S CHAPEL, OXFORD. Folio, 3s. 6d.
A small Chapel in the Early Perpendicular style. Size, 24 feet by 16. Estimated cost, 256l. Holds 90 persons.

STRIXTON CHURCH. Folio, 5s.
A small Church in the Early English style. Calculated for 200 persons; Cost about 800l.

OXFORD BURIAL-GROUND CHAPELS. Folio, 10s. 6d.
1. Norman.   2. Early English.   3. Decorated.
Separately, each 5s.

PUBLISHED BY THE OXFORD ARCHITECTURAL SOCIETY.
Sixpence per Sheet.

OPEN SEATS.
2. Haseley.
3. Steeple Aston.
4. Stanton Harcourt; Ensham.
5. Littlemore.

PATTERNS OF BENCH ENDS.
6. Steeple Aston, Sheet 1.
7. Ditto. Sheet 2.

OAK STALLS.
8. Beauchamp Chapel.
9. Tallund, Beverley, &c.

FONTS.
10. Heckington, (*Decorated*).
11. Newenden, (*Norman*).

REREDOS.
12. St. Michael's, Oxford.

PULPITS.
15. Wolvercot, (*Perpendicular*).
16. Beaulieu, (*Decorated*).
17. St. Giles', Oxford, (*Decorated*); with Coombe, (*Perpendicular*).

SCREENS.
19. Dorchester and Stanton Harcourt.

STONE DESK.
20. Crowle Church, (*Norman*).

LICH GATES.
21—23. Beckenham, West Wickham, Pulborough, Boughton Monchelsea.

6

ARCHÆOLOGICAL WORKS.

THE CALENDAR OF THE PRAYER-BOOK IL-LUSTRATED. (Comprising the first portion of the "Calendar of the Anglican Church," illustrated, enlarged, and corrected.) With upwards of Two Hundred Engravings from Mediæval Works of Art. Fcap. 8vo., *Sixth Thousand*, ornamental cloth, 6*s*.

INVENTORY of FURNITURE and ORNAMENTS REMAINING IN ALL THE PARISH CHURCHES OF HERTFORDSHIRE in the last year of the Reign of King Edward the Sixth: Transcribed from the Original Records, by JOHN EDWIN CUSSANS, F.R.HIST.S. Crown 8vo., limp cloth, price 4*s*.

DOMESDAY BOOK, or the Great Survey of England of William the Conqueror, A.D. MLXXXVI. Facsimile of the part relating to Oxfordshire. Folio, cloth, price 8*s*.

THE TRACT "DE INVENTIONE SANCTÆ CRUCIS NOSTRÆ IN MONTE ACUTO ET DE DUCTIONE EJUSDEM APUD WALTHAM," now first printed from the Manuscript in the British Museum, with Introduction and Notes by WILLIAM STUBBS, M.A., Regius Professor of Modern History. Royal 8vo., uniform with the Works issued by the Master of the Rolls, (only 100 copies printed), price 5*s*.; Demy 8vo., 3*s*. 6*d*.

SKETCH OF THE LIFE OF WALTER DE MERTON, Lord High Chancellor of England, and Bishop of Rochester; Founder of Merton College. By EDMUND, Bishop of Nelson, New Zealand; late Fellow of Merton College. 8vo., 2*s*.

THE STORY OF THE "DOMUS DEI" OF PORTSMOUTH, commonly called the Royal Garrison Church. By H. P. WRIGHT, M.A., Chaplain to the Forces, and Chaplain to H.R.H. the Duke of Cambridge, K.G. Crown 8vo., with Photographic and other Illustrations. 5*s*.

A MANUAL for the STUDY of SEPULCHRAL SLABS and CROSSES of the MIDDLE AGES. By the Rev. EDWARD L. CUTTS, B.A. 8vo., illustrated by upwards of 300 Engravings. 6*s*.

THE PRIMEVAL ANTIQUITIES OF ENGLAND AND DENMARK COMPARED. By J. J. A. WORSAAE. Translated and applied to the illustration of similar remains in England, by W. J. THOMS, F.S.A., &c. With numerous Illustrations. 8vo., cloth, 5*s*.

ARCHÆOLOGICAL WORKS.

DESCRIPTIVE NOTICES OF SOME OF THE ANCIENT PAROCHIAL & COLLEGIATE CHURCHES OF SCOTLAND, with Woodcuts by O. Jewitt. 8vo., 5s.

ARCHÆOLOGIA CAMBRENSIS, the Journal of the Cambrian Archæological Association. Vols. I., II., and III., Fourth Series. 8vo., cloth, each 1l. 10s.

OUR ENGLISH HOME: Its Early History and Progress. With Notes on the Introduction of Domestic Inventions. Third Edition. Crown 8vo., price 5s.

ART APPLIED TO INDUSTRY: A Series of Lectures by WILLIAM BURGES, F.R.I.B.A. Medium 8vo., cloth, price 4s.

THE ARCHÆOLOGICAL JOURNAL. Published under the Direction of the Central Committee of the Archæological Institute of Great Britain and Ireland, for the Encouragement and Prosecution of Researches into the Arts and Monuments of the Early and Middle Ages. 5 vols. With numerous Illustrations. 8vo., cloth, 2l.

PROCEEDINGS OF THE ARCHÆOLOGICAL INSTITUTE AT WINCHESTER, 1845. 8vo., 10s. 6d.

MEMOIRS ILLUSTRATIVE OF THE HISTORY AND ANTIQUITIES OF THE COUNTY AND CITY OF YORK, communicated to the Archæological Institute of Great Britain and Ireland, July, 1846. With 134 Illustrations. 8vo., cloth, 10s. 6d.

MEMOIRS ILLUSTRATIVE OF THE HISTORY AND ANTIQUITIES OF THE COUNTY AND CITY OF OXFORD, communicated to the Archæological Institute, June, 1850. 8vo., cloth, with Illustrations, 10s. 6d.

PROCEEDINGS AT NORWICH, 1847. 8vo., 10s. 6d.

THE GENTLEMAN'S MAGAZINE from 1856 to 1865, (Vol. I. to Vol. XIX.,) containing ARTICLES on Archæology, History, Architecture, &c.—Unpublished Documents.—Proceedings of Antiquarian Societies, &c. 8vo., 16s. per vol.

www.ingramcontent.com/pod-product-compliance
Lightning Source LLC
Chambersburg PA
CBHW031830230426
43669CB00009B/1298